"Anita has encapsulated the essence of Gujarati women at their best. The contribution of UK's Gujarati women to British society is hugely inspirational and this book is perhaps one of the best portrayals of determined women willing to transform communities."

CB Patel, Editor - Asian Voice

"Reading these stories was both awe inspiring and emotional. These women have shown such great tenacity whilst achieving so much, despite such overwhelming circumstances and adversity. Their altruistic acts are a lesson to us all on the road to further change."

Mala Agarwal, MD – Athena Care Homes

"I know from my own family the incredible power and inspiration of Gujarati women - it is so wonderful to see some of them celebrated here. In these 21 profiles we find the voices and experiences of so many other women all over the world, whose stories and names we may never know, but whose lives we will undoubtedly recognise."

Sonal Sachdev Patel, CEO - GMSP Foundation

"There is hidden power inside every woman and Anita brings these twenty-one stories to life in this book. Women's power is collective and though their expressed individuality, we can hear about their personal narratives to understand different perspectives to create positive impact together."

Mirela Sula, CEO - Global Woman Magazine and Global Woman Club

"As a daughter from a Gujarati family that had emigrated twice, firstly my grandparents from Gujarat to Kenya, then my parents to England. I can relate very strongly to the women featured in this book, Voices from Gujarat.

Language barriers, cultural barriers, the food and climate; everything is different from what these women grew up with. The same is said for my husband's family. My in laws came from Gujarat to the UK, where they built a successful publishing empire. Both sets of families made England their home and thrived. Overcoming hardships and learning to live a different type of lifestyle and making the best of both worlds. Both my mother and mother-in-law worked long hours, while still looking after a young family and elderly parents and in laws.

Growing up with these adaptable Gujarati women, has given us all a peek into how to live life with a multi-generational family and how to create our own destinies, through sheer hard work and grit.

Voices from Gujarat touches on these incredible women from Gujarat who had to make a life for themselves and realise their dreams, inspiring the next generation along the way."

Rashmita Solanki, Eastern Eye

"If you loved Voices from Punjab, then this is book is for you! Anita has interviewed prominent British Gujarati women leading their lives purposefully, with a vision to create gender equality. The heart-warming stories will lift your spirit as the women share their ancestral journey over three continents."

Jo Davison, Entrepreneur and Author

"Anita Goyal is an extraordinary woman, her vision to champion women and showcase the hidden stories of Indian women in particular is to be lauded. In 'Voices from Gujarat' she has captured the empowering and inspirational stories of second and third generation Gujarati women who have overcome adversity to forge successful careers and lives in Britain. I applaud the book and encourage more hidden stories to be highlighted in the series."

Lopa Patel MBE, Chair of Diversity UK

This is Anita's second book, which defines the true power of Asian women fighting for their rights. Anita is a pioneer for India women. The East Africa route adds a further dimension to Voices from Gujarat. I am looking forward to more work from her. This book is a great inspiring read.

Anil Gupta - Author, Speaker and Mentor

Voices from Gujarat

EMPOWERING STORIES OF 21 GUJARATI WOMEN TRANSFORMING BRITAIN

ANITA GOYAL MBE

CONTENTS

CHAPTER

11

LAVINA MEHTA MBE

Feel Good with Lavina

Page: 177

CHAPTER

12

HEENA SHAH

Pure Soul

Page: 177

CHAPTER

13

NINA AMIN MBE

Accountancy to Accolades

Page: 217

CHAPTER
14
TRUPTI PATEL
Dharmic Life
Page: 233

CHAPTER
15
VARSHA MISTRY
Defining Moment
Page: 249

CHAPTER
16
HEERAL SHAH
Spinning Plates
Page: 267

With best wishes,

Dedicated to my husband, Avnish Goyal

My biggest champion

Anita Goyal

Foreword

Pinky Lilani CBE DL

Voices from Gujarat is a heart-warming collection of stories to uplift our spirit and nourish our soul. The stories in this publication demonstrate the best qualities we share as human beings: kindness, compassion, grace, forgiveness, generosity, faith and courage. It is a collection of wisdom on love, parenting, teaching, aspirations and the overcoming of obstacles.

The publication of this is timely indeed. It is clear, that despite women's increased engagement in public decision-making roles, equality is far off: women hold about 21 percent of ministerial positions globally, only three countries have 50 percent or more women in parliament, and 22 countries are headed by a woman. At the current rate of progress, gender equality will not be reached among Heads of Government until 2150, another 130 years.

The Global Health crisis has sharply demonstrated that men's voices dominate in almost every category of media coverage related to the coronavirus crisis and every topic with the exception of what are often seen as women's issues such as childcare. The economic shocks of the pandemic will be felt in the immediate and long term – and it will be women who will pay the highest price. Silence and powerlessness go hand in hand, therefore the importance of women having a voice and being part of the narrative is more crucial than ever.

From time immemorial women have been the backbone of society, it is they, who knit together the fabric of our communities, but for far too long their voices were not heard and their impact relegated to being mothers, wives, daughters or playing other supporting roles. The way in which women navigate life and leadership roles is unique: women have the capacity to love and nurture, coupled with an ability to prioritise and manage, qualities that directly translates to successful leadership.

With their fierce strength, they have the extraordinary ability to weave together a web of many details—essential to leadership at every level of society. Women's power is both collective, in nurturing development, and individual, using their personal narratives to understand others' perspectives and connect differences to create positive, holistic outcomes for those they encounter.

The women in this book hail from many different backgrounds and professions, what they share is a sense of purpose, a sense of fortitude to step outside their comfort zone and act despite any fears and insecurities they may have, in a society that is often conflicted about how women should exercise authority, if at all. Sharing stories is crucial.

The importance of storytelling is paramount. Storytelling is universal and is as ancient as humankind. Before there was writing, there was storytelling. It occurs in every culture and from every age. It exists (and existed) to entertain, to inform, and to promulgate cultural traditions and values. Through the ages it took many different forms from oral recitation to drawings, paintings, dance and puppetry.

Story telling in India has a particularly rich heritage, it was a way of preserving the culture and beliefs of a tribe or community. Anita Goyal is continuing this rich tradition. She is ultimately an admirable storyteller, she has used her exceptional skills to connect women to a larger purpose. Voices from Gujarat gives us hope that we can build a society that gives women choices – to be whatever they may dream of, to be part of a community that enables them, motivates them to break glass ceilings and pave their own paths whilst lifting others too. Because when women lead, we all do better.

Pinky Lilani CBE DL

Founder and Chair of Women of the Future Awards and the Asian Women of Achievement Awards

Introduction

ANITA GOYAL MBE

Back in 2011, when I lost my first husband to a chronic illness, I was blessed with phenomenal support from my family and friends. Almost three hundred people attended his funeral to pay their last respects. I was thirty-eight years old and together with my thirteen-year-old daughter we grieved our loss. That was a dark time for us, and I don't know how my days flowed as I went through the pain.

In 2020 and 2021, many thousands of women and men lost loved ones to Covid-19, including some of my friends, widowed at a young age and left to cope in bleak circumstances. No-one could have predicted what was in store for these women and I acknowledge them for persevering through their adversity and days of despair.

Here in this book, I want to celebrate and share the voices of women during these times. Building on my earlier publication Voices from Punjab, this book is an opportunity to search and find Gujarati women, to inhabit their world and represent it to you - the reader. It gives us a window into these women's hearts, souls, and minds. My curiosity and interest in sharing the stories of more phenomenal British Asian women is a privilege and joy.

Voices from Gujarat is a collection of twenty-one stories of women with heritage from Gujarat, the northwest Indian state rich in history and tradition. Each woman has something unique to share: every life experience has been so personal, and their messages are equally distinct. The twenty-one stories are woven together to bring shared values of culture, language, and upbringing, acknowledging their similarities, and embracing their differences in the communities we live in today.

For many, their family history is marked by a double emigration: first from Gujarat to East Africa and then, after political turbulence in the 1960s and 1970s, from countries such as Kenya, Uganda and Tanzania to Britain. As some of the women remark, Gujarati society in the UK has parallels with Jewish communities: both have experienced dislocations and migrations across continents, binding their extended families and strengthening their culture. These migrations also created a special resilience among Gujarati families, as they committed themselves to work hard, to realise their dreams and contribute to the society around them. I was determined to find out more about how Gujarati women in Britain live today.

I started my journey by arranging to meet these phenomenal women over a coffee in London, diving into their world and listening to their story and messages. With the national lockdowns in the UK in March, I diverted my interviews to take place on the phenomenal Zoom! This enabled me to reach out to even more great women, like Shivali Bhammer who was living in the US at the time. Shivali, in her chapter 'Flow Like a River' followed her dream of being a singer having entered the competitive Bollywood scene, her trials and tribulations combine with a devotion to her spirituality.

As the unprecedented pandemic unfolded, it became apparent that some of these women were transforming their work around Covid-19 and engaging communities, causing a paradigm shift. One such woman was Lavina Mehta MBE. I was so delighted when Lavina was recognised for her work, and in October 2020 she was awarded an MBE for services to health and fitness during Covid-19. Her mission is to help people feel good, physically, mentally and emotionally. She passionately promotes the health benefits of exercise on TV and radio, including her ingenious concept of 'Exercise Snacking'. During lockdown she provided free twice-daily virtual workouts with her family, for all ages, and continues to provide specially designed virtual chair workouts to help thousands of elderly and vulnerable people stay fit, physically and mentally, from their homes. Her slogan is: "Exercise for Sanity not Vanity" and she is a powerful advocate of the mental health benefits of exercise.

I interviewed powerlifter, judo black belt and former MMA fighter, Ameesha Bhudia, who now works as a martial arts coach - teaching children to defend themselves. More recently she became the first Gujarati female in the London Fire Brigade! Ameesha told me how her fascination for judo began and how this led to her competing in the boy's category during a tournament in Paris and the struggles she's faced as a female fighter and as an Asian woman.

Hearing stories of Gujarati women in sport is really important for the next generation wishing to embark on a completely different path. We have the privilege to read about Naomi Dattani's life, a professional cricketer of Gujarati heritage in the UK, in her chapter 'Cricket Craze.' Naomi's story shares the sacrifice she's made to pursue her dreams. Her message of setting goals to optimise her life are applicable to all, especially with her volunteering roles. She reflects on how sport can be used to unite gangs, relating how a south African charity - Balls for Poverty - demonstrated how sport literally persuaded gangs to put their guns down!

Nishma Gosrani OBE is truly inspirational: she's passionate about equality and inclusion in the workplace. Nishma was invested with an OBE in Her Majesty's 2020 Honours List for her work pioneering Gender Pay Gap reporting, which led to changes in the Equality Act. In her chapter 'The Blue Sari', we discover how the leadership qualities of her grandmother influenced Nishma in a profound way. Her grandmother's entrepreneurial spirit surfaced from selling homemade chutney in the local markets in Nairobi, Kenya. Over time, her mission to contribute to her family grew into an empire. The essence of this story is about how love drives you to take action from loss, a story that brings me to tears every time I read it!

Another outstanding woman, driving change is Dr Yoge Patel in her chapter 'Flying High'. Yoge is the Chief Executive Officer of the Blue Bear Group and an authoritative and respected figure in the Aerospace and Maritime Industry. Her calm manner and simplicity is a reflection of the humble upbringing she had in Mombasa, Kenya. I was fascinated by her journey in the exciting and competitive world of Artificial Intelligence. In her chapter 'Defining Moment,' Zambian born Varsha Mistry was the only woman of colour at her police station when first posted as a crime scene examiner in the 1980s. Varsha shares the difficulties she encountered in England. She also told me about the great strides towards inclusivity in the police service, some of which she helped to make. Ever since a near-death experience irrevocably changed her life, Varsha has volunteered on several projects, including serving as the first female chairperson for the Met Police Hindu Association and as regional director of Hindu Council UK.

A pioneer in broadcasting, leading the way for other journalists, Sonali Shah is a regular face on BBC One and has been on screen for almost fourteen years. She's in her eighth year of hosting the property show Escape to the Country and also presents many live events for the BBC, such as Trooping the Colour, The Lord Mayor's Show and The Commonwealth Service. Sonali gives us insight into being a journalist and, the 'unofficial agreement' between her and her father while pursuing a not-so-regular career. In her chapter 'Solidarity in Solitude', she dives into her experiences at the BBC, the skills she's needed and reflects on her attitude going into dangerous situations such reporting from Afghanistan. Sonali gives us a fascinating insight into how the pandemic has impacted the public.

Be inspired by Nisha Parmar's captivating story about the courage and strength needed to follow her life passion of cooking. This was cemented by her achievement as a semi-finalist 2018 on BBC's MasterChef. In her chapter 'Nourish Your Soul,' we discover how her decisions have shaped her becoming a celebrity chef with an Instagram following of more than seventy-four thousand people! Discover how her life has changed following her decision to quit her job as a banker. This was the second major decision of her life with a profound impact on her journey: find out what her first one was!

We read of the strength that Panna Vekeria showed when she was faced by an early menopause in her thirties and how she resolved to have her own children. This is one of the greatest steps that I think a woman can take in her life. She smashed through taboos, starting first by joining the Army and then becoming a single mum of two children. Discover in her chapter 'Odds Against Time,' how she encountered all the challenges and overcame them with her tenacity and spirit.

Hansa Pankania is an author of several books and a counsellor with a focus on stress management. She was so inspired by Deepak Chopra's work at his wellness centre in California that she set up her own wellbeing hub – Aum - and became the first entrepreneur in her family. In her chapter, 'Oneness with the world,' Hansa takes us on a journey of becoming mindful to manage mental health and shares her personal and professional perspective on this vital topic, especially relevant for children today.

As you read these stories, you'll be surprised to see how many difficulties women have faced through the generations. I was particularly astonished when Kamu Palan shared in her chapter 'Touring London,' how her mother was married aged eleven as a child bride from

Gujarat and gave birth to her first child at the tender age of fifteen! Kamu adores her mother and all the adversities that they faced as a family growing up in Tanzania. From the moment she arrived in the UK, her hard work and determination and ingenuity led her to run various businesses with her husband. They made and sold bespoke crisps to Harrods and eventually set up Golden Tours in London, with their unmistakeable blue open top tourist buses.

I was intrigued to learn about Krishna Pujara in her chapter 'Global Woman,' from her beginnings in an adoring family in Tanzania. When she arrived in the UK, she embarked upon a successful career in the eighties, whizzing around London in her red convertible Mercedes. She began working in a financial company and became a wealth consultant, but everything changed after she got married and moved to Kenya. Her story makes the point that freedom is more precious that the finer things in life.

Heena Shah shared her tragic story of the loss at thirty-eight weeks of her second child, her beautiful daughter. In her chapter 'Pure Soul,' there isn't satisfactory explanation, and she will never be able be to replace her loss, although Heena shows a huge amount of strength to care for her eldest daughter and younger son. In the UK, around 5000 babies are stillborn or die within the first four weeks of their lives. This makes up 75 per cent of the deaths of children under the age of 16. It is still not understood why many babies die, or what more can be done to prevent them. This was Heena's pain, as she sought to understand what really happened. As I have discussed with so many women, it is still taboo in some cultures to talk about miscarriage or stillbirth and they are still linked to stigma and shame. I am so grateful that through Heena's story, we can be inspired to raise awareness and support women who have gone through these experiences.

Nina Amin MBE left Kenya aged seventeen in pursuit of her dream of becoming an accountant. Her counterparts assumed that she had failed her exams only to realise that she had passed with flying colours. Working in a firm that didn't recognise her true value as a fully qualified accountant and keeping her on a training contract salary reveals how gender inequalities were so prevalent in society in the 1970s. In her chapter 'Accountancy to Accolades,' she details the values and dedication needed to achieve the heights that Nina has reached. Trupti Patel from Gujarat experienced similar prejudices as a qualified civil engineer, being Asian and a woman in a sector that was dominated by men. Despite being pushed aside, Trupti stood her ground and succeeded in leading major projects. 'Dharmic Life,' celebrates the life of a woman born in the heart of Gujarat who has contributed to British Asian life. Women like Nina and Trupti have paved the way for the next generation so that we are not confronted with the same inequalities that they have experienced.

Nishma Gosrani OBE strives to extend the progress of equality in the workplace, especially for Asian women, in the hope that the next generation will be able to thrive without any barriers that colour currently presents. There is still much work to be done before we can say that we live in a balanced world. Another person working on this is Minal Mehta. In her chapter 'Achievers Mindset,' we learn about her gap year achievements where her messages focus on amplifying diversity. Working with musicians and producers, she tackles issues such as gender inequality and global climate change by using music as a communication tool to pursue her passion.

Heeral Shah, in her chapter 'Spinning Plates,' addresses the complexities of managing multiple responsibilities, as so many women do. She is a leader in the fast-paced world of banking, despite having taken breaks to have two children: she explains the many challenges this entails. As part of the Black Lives Matter movement, Heeral contributes to the Race at Work taskforce, where she has led this agenda for Barclays Corporate Banking, encouraging efforts to attract, develop, advance and retain Black, Asian and ethnic minority professionals.

The National Health Service (NHS) in the UK has been under immense strain during the series of national lockdowns, with successive surges in coronavirus cases. Doctors like Trisha Radia must be recognised and commended for their work. Dr Radia is a consultant paediatrician in London, where her work as a Training Programme Director means learning from incidents in hospital. Her passion for studying medicine began at an early age and later she determined to become a paediatrician. Trisha gives us insights into how she manages to balance the needs of her career, children, husband and extended family and friends. Both Trisha and Heeral are incredibly inspiring.

Loss can feature in so many ways especially through death and divorce. Much pain results and our true strength is revealed during this time. Through Kalpana Doshi's life story we learn about how divorce impacts confidence and self-belief. In her chapter 'A Liberated Woman,' she shares her perspective on how she led a lavish lifestyle with her first husband, but with strings attached and how she finally knew that the relationship had to end. Her daughter from her second marriage is her pride and joy, and she is strong and resilient in being a single mum, raising an exceptional young woman. Discover how Kalpana uses laughter yoga techniques and spirituality to thrive.

The death of Chandni Vora's mother at a young age is a story of love and loss. She has had great values bestowed upon her, giving her a distinct voice. This powerful story celebrates how a child can have many mothers committed to raising them. Chandni is a woman who sees the best in every person and situation and strives for excellence in everything she does. Her chapter, 'Gifts from my Mothers,' presents a dimension of womanhood that is rare in most cultures; her story is indeed a gift to us all.

Voices from Gujarat is a celebration of the phenomenal stories of these twenty-one Gujarati women. From OBEs to pioneering broadcast journalists, through to doctors, chefs and authors, these prominent women are brought together through their shared values of culture, language and upbringing. They are women who take charge of their happiness, recognise the power of resilience and hard work, and who strive to overcome the expectations placed upon them by society to achieve their dreams.

Many of the stories touch on the expectations of women within the Gujarati community, whether that is in their career or their personal life. The women reflect on the values instilled by their families and how their upbringing in a mixed Gujarati-British culture has shaped their approach to life, empowering them to break new ground and encouraging others in the process. Dealing with the complexities of a dual identity and maintaining a work-life balance, their stories also serve to show the sacrifices made by these women and those who came before them to pave the way for future generations.

Opening a window into their lives, you will accompany each woman on their journey as they prevail over gender stereotypes, cultural differences and the limited narratives written for them by stereotyped cultural attitudes of some in the Gujarati community. *Voices from Gujarat* will leave you with twenty-one new role models and the self-belief that you need to drive change, succeed against the odds and defy expectations. My heartfelt gratitude to these phenomenal women.

CHAPTER 1

Nourish your Soul

NISHA PARMAR

After spending seventeen arduous years working in investment banking, an industry that was stifling Nisha's creative soul, her life-changing moment occurred when her husband Sachin convinced her to apply to go on the BBC's MasterChef UK. Her modern approach to Indian cooking was soon noticed, and amazingly she made the semi-finals in

2018! Following the show, she started a business catering for private dinner parties, building her brand and being contracted by celebrities to provide unique dining experiences with her exquisite glamour and style. Her everyday dishes can also be savoured at her two cafés – The Secret Garden and Nourish by Nisha set in the modern Northwood gym in London.

*

It takes a powerful, brave person to take the course of their lives into their own hands and walk away from a familiar path when change is needed. If you don't change something yourself, nothing will change. Twice in my life, I have made huge adjustments to my own path when things no longer felt right for me - these aren't decisions I have made lightly, and I have worked hard to be successful in spite of venturing down new, unexpected routes.

Before I entered MasterChef, I had been working as a private banker in Canary Wharf. When I finished as a semi-finalist in the intense competition, I was devastated for a few weeks, but I quickly realised I could turn this experience into something more; after getting a taste of doing something I really loved, I couldn't let finishing as a semi-finalist be the end of my cooking career. As soon as I left the competition, my colleague asked me if I would cook dinner at their house, and after putting the dinner party pictures on Instagram, I started to get more and more requests from other people who wanted me to cook private dinners for them. While still working five days a week as a banker, I started cooking nearly every Saturday night for different groups. All of this extra work was the beginning of my journey towards becoming the owner of a private dining business, and my own cafes.

After every single dinner party, I would post pictures on Instagram. Within a short time, I was noticed by local celebrities, Tom and Giovanna Fletcher, who asked if I would like to cook for them. Pictures of the dinner I made for them went viral in their circle, and I started cooking for more celebrities including Joe Wicks, Ellie Goulding, Rochelle Humes and John Terry. I always use social media to show beautiful pictures of the food I make, which is a great way to promote my business. I know that when people really like the dishes I've made, they will share these pictures with others. I think being successful on social media means being your authentic self and writing to your followers as if you were having a conversation. In my posts, I am not writing like I am a business, I am writing naturally and authentically - I am showing my real personality with no filter.

As a private dining chef, I do everything myself - I do my accounts, I create my menus, I shop to source all the ingredients and carry all the materials and food to load up the car to transport to the various venues. I have a small team of two for the private dining experiences, but the cooking is one hundred percent me, and I publicly promote my work single handedly. But this is what I love doing, it's my passion so I am motivated easily to do all these tasks. I don't shy away from hard work.

I now run my own cafes, The Secret Garden and Nourish by Nisha, where I cook food I make at home for my own family, food which is welcoming and warming for the soul. It's located in the Northwood Club Private Gym in Northwood and it gives me an opportunity to be around a lot of people, talking to all kinds of new people who come into the cafe and experience healthy food. It was a massive risk when I decided to quit my banking job and embrace my cooking career at full speed, but it was a risk which has made my life so much better. Having my husband Sachin encouraging me made it slightly easier: he was confident I would excel and be happier as a chef.

I think there is an element of being brave and thinking: "Right, I have got to go with my gut instinct." Time moves so fast, and if you know something is not working for you, in whatever capacity, whether it is your job, your home life, the country you live in, if it's not working for you, you have to make the effort to change it.

When I was a banker, I woke up at five am before my children were up, and was on the Jubilee line by six am. By the time I got back home in the evenings, it was already very late and I would put my children to bed. Even though I would turn up with a smile on my face and do my best, I hated the job I was doing. I would sit at my desk and just get on with it, but I was so unhappy. From Sunday to Thursday, my job would put me in a bad mood and it affected my relationship with my family, as they could see how unhappy I was. Going on MasterChef made me realise I had to continue following my passion, but switching to working as a private chef was not a decision I could make lightly, as I had my husband and my two children to consider. It was a huge choice for our family, and we had a lot to think about financially. I wouldn't tell anyone to jump ship quickly, especially if they have children, and my choice meant calculating the financial risks and ensuring I had the safety nets in place for me and my family.

I am one hundred percent a different person now; my outlook on life is completely different. I have a much more determined mindset, and I never thought I was inspirational, but people are inspired by seeing me as a chef, doing what I love. I can spread more happiness because I am happier. My husband is always behind me, pushing me forward and this has spurred me on to try as hard as I can on my new career path. He is not fazed if there isn't dinner made for him on the table when he gets home or if I am busy all week, he just wants me to be happy. He wants me to get out there as much as possible. He was the one that encouraged me to complete the application for the MasterChef competition, as he believed in me more than I did at that time. I think some men are a bit intimidated by a strong, powerful woman who is being successful on their own, but I feel very lucky that I have a great husband who supports me through everything and embraces my successes.

Food was an essential part of our household when I was growing up, as I think is similar in most Asian cultures. My parents are both from Gujarat originally, although my dad was born and raised in Mombasa, Kenya, while my mother grew up in Jamnager, Gujarat. They got married in 1978, and moved to England, where nearly all of our neighbours were also Indian. Both of my parents worked incredibly hard - my dad was an accountant, and my mum worked in manual labour in a factory. We didn't have much money, but we enjoyed life. Relatives were frequently round to eat at our house, and we would share our meals together. When I started school at age three, I was a pure Gujarati girl - I didn't speak any English, and I had to pick it up during my lessons. My parents and I always spoke in Gujarati together, and I spoke often with my mum about her relatives in Gujarat, who still live in the same house she grew up in. I remember being so excited every time I came home to see my mum had received blue airmail letters from our family in Gujarat. When we opened the letters, the first thing we would do is smell them - they smelled just like India. My mum would read the letters to me, and then I would try and read them too, which helped improve my Gujarati. These were some of my fondest memories, because my mum had two sisters and three brothers in India, so we would get to read about their lives in Gujarat, and then I sat with my mum while she would write back to them. It was a wonderful way to stay connected. These tiny little childhood pleasures become memories which live on in your mind and heart forever.

I am brown and proud. My colour does not limit me; I think my colour is my advantage. Even when I was working as a banker, I didn't see being Indian as a disadvantage - I think sometimes people think that because they are Indian they won't progress as much, but we have the chance to push past this stereotype and show how much we can achieve. I have always been proud of my heritage and vocal about the Indian traditions that I am a part of: I love my Indian clothes, music, and food, my culture is so enriched. Sometimes it doesn't come naturally to people, but I think if you can, be proud of your heritage and use it to your advantage. It is so beautiful to be a part of two cultures, there is so much we can learn from both and I think now is the time to take advantage of that. When I was on MasterChef, I once heard someone say that I was going to go far because I was Indian and I remember thinking, that people would like me just because I am Indian, nonetheless it may have meant people were feeling intimidated by me in this competition. I felt I was being noticed for the right reasons, and recognised for how much I could contribute.

It was hard to convince my family, especially my dad, as he had put me through university, that giving up a solid career to become a chef was a good idea. They thought I was making a poor decision. I was worried that I would not only be letting myself down but my parents too, and there was pressure for me to succeed. But my gut instinct told me this was what I needed to do, even if I had doubts in my mind, I needed to push forward and dispel the negative thoughts. Now, they are very proud of me and what I have achieved as a cook, and they can see I am much happier.

This wasn't the first time I had to convince my parents of a huge change in the direction of my life. When I was twenty-four, I decided to divorce my first husband, a choice which my parents did not approve of, as they believed marriage was for life. I married my first husband when I was twenty-one, but it was an awful marriage. Marrying him was the worst thing I ever did. He would behave appallingly all the time and cheat on me often. I was so unhappy, but at the time I had no idea about a lot of the terrible things he did because I was working in the city. I had an amazing job, I was getting flown to Monaco by helicopter, staying in flashy hotels, working as a banker looking after millionaires. I didn't comprehend what was going on back home because work was so busy and the social parts of work would go on all night. Then, I think by fate, I suddenly caught him cheating - this was my excuse to get out.

When I told my parents I wanted a divorce, they said I wasn't allowed. They had invested so much money into a huge wedding, and they worried about what people would think when they found out the marriage was over and how it would impact my reputation and honour of the family. I was adamant and decided I was going to get a divorce anyway, so I went to find a lawyer and started the process. It was a powerful decision which my parents are very happy with now, as they could see how much pressure had been alleviated.

Though we have had some occasional disagreements, both of my parents are very inspirational for me. My mother moved to England when she was still quite young, and after arriving with her own beliefs and values, she had to quickly grow to understand a new culture. It was hard for her in our family, because when I was a baby we still lived with my dad's younger sisters, my aunts, who were teenagers. They had a very complicated relationship with my mum, and they treated her terribly. She was completely disrespected by her sisters-in-law, who would tease her for wearing a sari or having oily hair, as she was used to a completely different way of life than that of England. She was unhappy for a long time, but both sisters moved out eventually. I think it made me stronger watching her strength. You would never be able to notice the torment she experienced as she is always the world's happiest person. Even after going through so much in her life, including having breast cancer, she is the most friendly, kind and compassionate person. She's always smiling and chatting; she is incredible to me. Her mantra in life is always to have lots of fun, and not to take life too seriously, just be happy and enjoy whatever you can.

For my dad, things have not been easy either. He came from a poor family, but he was very clever in school so his parents pushed him to study hard. But then, when he was seventeen, he was burned very badly - he had about seventy-five percent of his body in need of skin grafts and they worried he might die. I think when he had the opportunity to come to the UK after he recovered, he saw it as a chance to start a new life. Recently, when we were on holiday he decided to wear shorts and swim with us. He's told me that in the past in Mombasa, he would swim all the time, and now he has built up the courage thirty years after his injuries to feel he can get back into the sea again. He's grown confidence in himself and feels comfortable now. Watching both of my parents going through their traumas and overcoming such difficult experiences and taking everything in their stride has given me strength and shaped me into who I am today.

I felt revitalized after the marriage ended. This was my chance to do everything I wanted to without any inhibitions. At work, I went for every promotion I could and tried my hardest. I moved back in with my parents for a short time, but as a twenty-four-year old, I needed my own space and so I bought my own flat and got to experience life on my own for a while. Then, two years later, at a friend's birthday party by chance I started chatting with a man and told him everything I was going through, and he really helped me. It was at a point in my life when I didn't feel like I needed anybody, but I connected with Sachin like I haven't with anyone else, it may sound clichéd, but I knew he was my soul mate.

When I got married to Sachin at twenty-nine, I was much more certain of myself and I had the ability to make good decisions. I felt strong and confident in myself, which I think is key. I believe your twenties are time for your own self-development. Before you approach your thirties, there is still so much you need to learn about yourself. If I look back, I'm glad my first marriage happened because it has made me stronger, but I do think that twenties are a time to get to know yourself and develop your career. If you don't know yourself properly, how can you get to know somebody else? Perhaps often, we look for safety and security when we look for a partner, but we need to find confidence within ourselves instead of trying to get it from others. If you can survive alone, then having somebody else to compliment you is going to help you excel. Getting married is not a comfort blanket - it is one of the hardest things ever. Being able to compromise and create a life with someone else is tough, and you need the ability to know yourself and to empathise with others.

Taking the time to learn about ourselves also means we can learn about what brings us joy and makes us feel relaxed: it's so important to make that time for ourselves to indulge in our hobbies, in the things which make us happy. Even if it's just for an hour, I try to set aside time for myself to just switch off and do something purely for me. If you enjoy sewing or art, make that time for yourself, because nobody else is going to make it for you. We all deserve to give ourselves that time to indulge in our passions.

When I used to work at Canary Wharf, on lunch breaks I would buy so many things just for the sake of buying things, because I was so exhausted and I thought shopping might make me feel better - in reality, I was just exhausted from all of the intense work, and I needed a change of career not to fill the void by shopping. I enjoy my profession much more, and so finding my inner peace is a lot easier. Shopping the way I used to is just not part of my life anymore, and I try to just focus on moments of tranquility I can find in my day-to-day life, moments which I can relax in without being materialistic. Even with so much to do all the time, I try nonetheless to find moments for myself, to do exercise like Pilates or cardio, because staying in shape makes me feel much better. When I have an hour to myself, I love to sit down quietly with a cup of tea and flick through food magazines or books, or turn the TV on and watch something, or research where we can go on our next holiday. My work involves being around people a lot, so it's important I have these moments to enjoy my own company. I believe everybody should set aside some time to be with themselves. These small forms of self-care may not seem like a lot, but they make all the difference.

As I look into the future for my career, I would love to have my own cooking TV show. While I think there is a lot of open space for British Asian chefs on TV, I think people sometimes expect me to cook Indian food because I am an Indian woman - this stereotyping is of course inaccurate, because I don't just cook Indian food and I don't just eat curries. Growing up as a British Indian child, I was always interested in food and the differences between the Gujarati food I had at home with my parents, and the food I was given to eat at my English school. I remember wanting to explore other types of food. I want my cooking to reflect my own authentic cooking style, which is a modern approach to Indian cuisine but is also inspired by a variety of other cuisines. I have an appreciation for so many different flavours and styles, particularly inspired by my travels in the Far East. At the moment, I am looking forward to creating recipes for a new initiative set up by Greg Wallace, one of the MasterChef judges, and I was invited back to MasterChef as a judge, which was really exciting as usually people are only invited back if they are winners or finalists. I think it is the ultimate compliment to have been invited back to judge the competition, because it means I am trusted completely in my judgement as a chef.

CHAPTER 2

Solidarity in Solitude

SONALI SHAH

Sonali Shah is a journalist and broadcaster who has presented shows across the BBC. She started as a business reporter, went on to host Newsround and became part of the presentation teams for BBC Sport and BBC Events, covering the Commonwealth Games in Delhi and London 2012. She currently hosts Escape to the Country and live events on BBC One and reports for ITV Tonight. During our interview, Sonali spoke about her experience as a working mother and balancing home and work life. She emphasised the importance of family and shared the dilemmas that many parents raising children in the modern age face. She discussed her heritage as a British woman with Gujarati culture and parents who grew up in East Africa, underlining the changes we still need to make in workplaces and across society, in our efforts to reach equality.

*

When I went to Afghanistan to film some BBC documentaries on children growing up in a warzone, my family had real mixed feelings - they knew how important my work was to me, but weren't thrilled about where I was going. When I was asked to return a few months later, I reluctantly said no because my family had been so worried the first time around. I had gone through hostile training and participated in briefings about what to do if I was kidnapped, and I couldn't put my family through all of that again so soon. Life is always about balance and, in that moment, it made more sense to me to put family first.

When I chose to study journalism as a fresh-faced seventeen-year-old, I remember people around me thinking it was a bit strange, perhaps a bit left-field. In our Gujarati community in the late nineties, most people didn't know anyone who had entered the media arena. Some assumed I must have performed poorly in my A-Levels. The truth was I had achieved three A's in biology, chemistry and psychology and my mum had nudged me to try something different. Picking a career outside the medical field must have seemed unusual at the time, especially as my mother was a midwife and my father was a pharmacist. But we can't be afraid to go down new paths – it's important we are represented in all parts of society.

In our youth, it can be difficult to make important decisions about our future. Of course, we are all influenced by what we see around us. As my family had largely taken the science route and I loved science at school, I thought it would be the right path for me too – I wanted to be a doctor. My attempt to obtain experience in that area, while still in school, led me to volunteer at a local hospital radio station. Little did I know at the time that this was the beginning of my journalism career – sparking my interest in presenting.

Nowadays, it seems everyone wants to become a presenter, but when I started down this path more than twenty years ago, things felt different. The media landscape has changed dramatically over the years. Modern technology and social media mean you can create your own content and build an online presence without needing the help of a traditional broadcaster to enter this field - these options just didn't exist when I studied journalism. The positive aspect of this development has been allowing people from different backgrounds to try to make a name for themselves – which hasn't always happen in traditional media. The industry may have expanded but we need to make larger strides towards equality. There may be a number of non-white people fronting programmes now, but companies need to employ more people from different backgrounds behind the scenes, making editorial decisions and having an input on who to hire. I still hear so many stories of non-white journalists knowing they have had to be twice as good at their job as their white counterpart, to prove that they're worthy of a certain position.

Being a working parent is a constant juggling act. Sometimes, I've been asked: "Are your children okay with you being away from home for work?" Yes my children miss me, but when I am away, they get to spend quality time with their grandparents, and be spoiled by them. This arrangement is all they've ever known. It really is true that it takes a village to raise a child. In a way, we are living the extended family life just as our families used to in East Africa, except in our version we live in three different houses. That has enabled me to dedicate time not only to my job but also to some charity work. I always say that giving my time to charity is a donation from my family, not only me, because without someone else babysitting, I wouldn't have time to do it. I am an ambassador for Barnardo's, The Prince's Trust, and the British Asian Trust and also support Great Ormond Street Hospital.

Both sides of my family have Gujarati heritage, but my parents and in-laws were all born and grew up in East Africa. They tell me about the strong sense of solidarity they had with other Asian communities who had also moved to Africa. This spirit followed us to England: I was born and raised in London, I am a Brit, but I share close ties to my family's Gujarati heritage and the Jain faith which I was born into. I used to attend a Jain community youth club, and I've always had a group of close friends from the Gujarati community linking me to my heritage.

A huge part of our family community spirit is in cooking and feeding others. My mum and mother-in-law both learned to cook from their mothers and aunties, and this is being passed onto me and my husband; Gujarati food will always be comfort food for us. When we cook together as a family, it's a great time for bonding, and our daughter and son will watch us cook and participate when they can. Sharing food together with family is one of the great joys in life; we love to eat with our parents and pass all these incredible dishes around. I think we've inherited a Gujarati desire to share - if I cook, I don't just cook for my house, I'll cook two or three times that amount, and we'll take it over to family.

While I believe that family traditions can evolve as we question the ways things have been done in the past to think about how we might need to grow, one strong tradition our family still honours is vegetarianism. This comes from being born into the Jain community. While I'm not religious, many Jain principles are engrained in our way of life. The main principle of Jainism is Ahimsa, meaning non-violence. Not eating meat is part of that. Vegetarianism is now more popular in the Western world, but I do think you need quite an international palate, so you don't miss out on key nutrients. When I think about my grandparents growing up in Gujarat, they would have eaten dahl, a lentil-based dish, every day, meaning they would have always had protein. Now, though, in the UK, I often see that vegetarian substitutes for meat are made with a lot of processed ingredients, which isn't always ideal. That's why I find sticking to a Gujarati or Indian-based diet, helps me try to stay healthy.

The year 2020 was meant to be a celebration of me turning 40 – we'd planned lots of adventures with the children. It's now the year everyone will remember as the Year of Covid. At the beginning of the pandemic there was so much talk about how the virus 'doesn't discriminate'. There was an assumption that it was a leveller, that we were all in this together. But in reality, certain parts of society have been hit the hardest. Those who were struggling before have had to turn to foodbanks to feed their family. Businesses couldn't expect to thrive but just hope they survived. Those living on their own had to cope with being isolated. We all became aware of our mental health and wellbeing.

South Asians have also been disproportionately hit – and not all the reasons for that are known. But one is fairly obvious – there are so many people from our community working on the front line. My 67-year-old Dad has had to continue working as a pharmacist throughout the pandemic, despite our worries about this vulnerability. As usual, he has taken it all in his stride. It's been interesting to observe how people have had to pause during this time. It has forced us all to take stock of our lives – to figure out what is important to us, to realise who is important to us. There are so many family members we have reconnected with and that has been one of the positives of this time.

I'm lucky that I have been able to work during this time. We had to stop filming Escape to the Country which I had been doing for the past six years. But as a broadcast journalist, I was classed as a key worker which allowed me to work in news-related programming. I filmed for a programme for ITV Tonight called '*Lockdown: How Long Can It Last?'* The filming all took place in Manchester and I drove up from London to stay in a key worker hotel for two nights. Work has been possible through a combination of self-shooting videos at home on my mobile phone, conducting interviews via video call or making sure I'm standing two metres away from others when filming. For a VE Day broadcast for the Royal British Legion, they set everything up in a large film studio to keep everyone apart. For the Queen's Official Birthday, Trooping the Colour was cancelled but we were able to cover a smaller ceremony at Windsor Castle where the guardsmen learnt how to parade while social distancing.

My husband is involved in the hospitality sector and during the lockdown, everything had to close. It was heart-warming to see members of their team using their time to cook meals for NHS workers in London hospitals. It's been incredible to see generosity like this up and down the country, especially during a time of crisis, and I hope even simple acts like checking in on a neighbour continue when this is all over.

As a family who migrated from Gujarat to East Africa, we feel like a blended culture in some senses. Kenyan-Asian food is a sub-cuisine in itself and many restaurants around us have ingredients such as cassava as a result of our families living in Kenya, Tanzania and Uganda. When you move to a country, you have to integrate. My parents and my in-laws all speak Swahili and growing up I often used Swahili words under the assumption they were Gujarati. Our Gujarati culture is different to someone living in Gujarat (which was one of the divided states during Partition) now. In East Africa, Asian families stuck together as one community and were all neighbours regardless of their heritage. You could be next door to a Hindu, Muslim or Sikh family and there wasn't a divide, differences weren't prevalent.

My parents both moved to the UK to study when they were seventeen years old - they were both born under British rule. They've always worked incredibly hard and that taught me the value of hard work. It's only since becoming a parent that I have started to understand just how motivated and driven they were to do the best they could for their children. My father was sent to England by his family in Tanzania - he was given a small amount of money and told to go and make a life for himself - and as this was during the seventies he paid rent for a room to stay with a family while he was studying his A-Levels. As he couldn't afford two years of rent, he completed his A-Levels in just one year and then went to Bradford University to study pharmacy - he's owned his own pharmacy since my brother and I were little. At Bradford University, my father met my mother, who was studying nursing at the time. They got married in Kenya in 1977. My parents both worked as they raised my brother and me - because they didn't have much family here, they had to make it work without help. My mother was a midwife and a family planning nurse and she went back to work when I was six weeks old. She would work in the evenings, so some days my dad would arrive home just as my mum was leaving for work and they would just meet at the door. I've always been really lucky that my parents worked so hard to give me a happy childhood and a comfortable home.

I'm told we didn't really ask for much as children, and, because we were mostly surrounded by other families with similar financial situations to ours, I don't ever remember feeling like we were missing out on anything. Occasionally we worked in our dad's pharmacy, and he would give us some penny sweets, but we weren't given pocket money. I think that's what motivated me to find a job in my early teens and I haven't stopped working since. My parents are frugal – they've had to be in the past. They've often told me tales of when they first got together in the seventies, they wouldn't take the university bus back home because it cost three pence and they needed to save the money. Knowing stories like that helps me understand my parents a little more. My dad never has sugar in his tea, not because he doesn't have a sweet tooth, but because he simply couldn't afford sugar when he first lived in Britain. I think a small story like this tells me so much about my father and is a lesson perhaps my generation can learn from. Maybe we all have things in life which we think we need but could get used to living without.

I think that my generation values time more than money. When my mum wants to go to three different supermarkets to save money, or when my dad wants to drive fifteen minutes out of the way to go to a cheaper place to get petrol, I may laugh but I also know where those quirks come from. Time feels so precious to me now, more precious than money, and I think sometimes this can lead to impatience: I want things done fast. I'm learning more about being patient now that I have children, and also to understand my parents' resilience and strength.

As a parent, I want to make sure my children grow up with the same hunger that I had to succeed. We are trying to ensure that we don't spoil our children because of our own successes - our parents have worked extremely hard, we are working hard, and we have to manage how this transfers onto our children now, and ensure they understand the value of things they are given, and learn to stand on their own two feet.

As a working mother, I have occasionally felt guilty for not being with my children instead, but it's quickly shaken when my husband points out that he rarely feels like that. Maybe my guilt is rooted in society's expectations that women should be home with their children, or maybe it's just personality. Either way, I have that feeling less and less. I have built a life as a freelance presenter so that I can customise my schedule and balance the time I want to have with my children. Hopefully, I'm also instilling values that enable my children to thrive.

CHAPTER 3

My Beautiful Black Belt

AMEESHA BHUDIA

Ameesha was a Mixed Martial Artist (MMA) who trained and competed in judo, kickboxing, MMA (also known as cage fighting) and her most recent accomplishment, powerlifting. Ameesha is a dedicated sportswoman, and she has experienced her fair share of successes and struggles while practicing martial arts. At the age of twelve, she won bronze in the National Championships for Judo and began representing Great Britain as a part of the British squad. By age sixteen, she won gold at the Nationals and competed in the European Championships. With her strength, confidence, and ambition, in her late twenties Ameesha began competing in cage fights as an MMA fighter. She now works as a martial arts coach, teaching children to defend themselves, a gym manager and as a personal trainer, helping to empower other women as they gain confidence and strength in martial arts. As a young mother raising a son, Ameesha's story reveals how important staying active is for the mind and soul, and how vital it is to raise your children with a pure, non-judgmental heart.

*

Stepping into the cage against the famous Mixed Martial Arts Champion, Molly McCann, for my first MMA fight was not something I ever expected to do. Cage fighting always seemed too violent and aggressive for me. I never thought MMA could be my thing, but when I was twenty-seven years old, a friend of mine from work encouraged me to watch a fight show with him. I loved it. As I watched, I realised how much I wanted to get in the cage and fight. A fire sparked in me – I saw how the judo skills I'd been perfecting during my younger years could be used in the cage, and I even began planning my own strategies for fights. Straight away, I started training in more MMA-style fighting techniques; it was perfect, I could use my judo experience and also practice new things like kickboxing/K1, wrestling and Brazilian jiu-jitsu in order to become a strong, powerful fighter. I felt amazing – in training I'd spar against male fighters and was able to use my skills to throw them to the floor. When I fought in the cage against Molly, the rush was unbelievable. Even though I lost the fight, my powerful performance led to offers for more fights. I felt so proud – people told me I'd fought amazingly for my first time in the cage, and, as a major adrenaline junkie, I left with a hunger to train and become even stronger.

I have always been very passionate about training in judo; I enjoy having the power to defend myself. When I was a young girl, I was constantly filled with energy and my parents put me in lots of different classes to try and help me feel less hyperactive. I tried ballet, gymnastics, karate and even horse riding, but the one sport that really stuck for me was judo. From the age of eight, judo became my life. It's more of a contact sport than karate – during fights you throw each other around with the aim of getting your opponent flat on their back or pinning them to the floor – and I found this truly exciting and empowering. Within two weeks of starting judo, my coach put me into my first little local competition. Of course, I had no experience and I lost all of my fights, but as an eight-year-old girl I was just ecstatic to be involved. I was given a trophy for participation and I felt so happy and proud of myself. I took it into school the next day to show everyone.

I flew to Paris with my mum for my first ever international competition when I turned nine. I was quite a tomboy at the time – my hair was cut very short and I stuck to baggy trousers and t-shirts instead of dresses or skirts. When I arrived for the competition, I was weighed and put into a category for my weight class as per usual for judo competitions. But I soon realised something was wrong when I was called up to compete – there were only boys around me, and we found out I'd been mistaken for a boy and entered into the boys' category! The girls' category was over by the time we realised, so I had the choice to either compete with the boys or not compete at all. All the French boys were laughing at me when they heard I was actually a girl, but I didn't really care. I was only interested in winning, and I did. In the final, I was up against one of the boys who had been laughing at me and I made him cry in the final by throwing him flat on his back during our fight. Proving myself against the boys, I won the entire competition.

Straight after we finished the fight, my mum told me she was never going to come and watch again. She was horrified to see anyone hurting me even a little bit and told me she wanted to get up onto the mat and beat up anyone who I was competing with. So, she stopped coming to my competitions, and I found this worked better for both of us because I didn't have to worry about anyone watching me and could just get on with practicing judo. Nonetheless, my parents were always incredibly supportive of my judo training and almost any other part of my life which wasn't typical in our family community. I was born and raised in London, but my parents both have Gujarati heritage. My baa (grandmother) didn't like the idea of me going abroad at such a young age without my parents. The more religious side of my family were surprised my parents let me train and compete with boys – they didn't like the idea that nobody could monitor what I was doing, but my parents always believed in me.

My own parents allowing me to just be who I wanted to be helped me grow up with confidence in myself. Thinking back on it now, I watched both the women and men in our Gujarati community and noticed a distinct difference – the women spent the majority of their time in the kitchen and were expected to be the weaker sex and not lift things or do much manual work. I knew from a young age that this was not what I wanted. Training in judo was something I got a real thrill from and I loved being able to throw people around; this type of power wasn't expected of me as a girl, but it was what made me feel the most myself, so I pursued it. When I was a tomboy, I was much more in favour of being practical over anything else, and I never cared much about what anyone else might think. My mum fought my corner against those who weren't as understanding of my choice not to wear a pretty dress and to do a contact sport with boys. Of course, things have changed now, and although when I was growing up I missed a lot of family events for judo competitions, now I really enjoy getting dressed up with my son and attending the traditional ceremonies such as Diwali. Spending time with family and showing our appreciation for each other at these events is very important to me, and I am happy I can pass these traditions down to my son.

After my first international fight when I was nine, I began regularly competing. My whole life was devoted to my judo training – my coach was very determined for all of his students to compete, so I would travel to different competitions almost every weekend. Sometimes I would even compete back-to-back on Saturday and Sunday. By the age of twelve, I went to the National Championships and won the bronze medal, meaning I became third best at judo in the country in my age group. Winning a medal meant I was selected for the British squad. All of my hard work for judo training shone bright and clear as I started to represent Great Britain.

I think practicing judo also really helped me feel comfortable in my own skin. I knew I was strong and could defend myself against anything, and, more importantly, I knew I could use my strength to help other people. In school, other students would ask me to help them with problems they were having with bullies. It was well known at my school that I did martial arts, and I felt empowered to go and speak to bullies to try and stop the problems. I felt confident I could help by explaining to students why they shouldn't bully, and fortunately a lot of the time this worked very well, and the bullying would stop. I loved the strength I gained from practicing martial arts; one of my jobs now is to teach children martial arts, and I'm very passionate about making sure that all children should learn some form of martial arts because I think there are endless benefits to doing so.

Once I started representing Great Britain in the British squad for judo, I was determined to win a gold medal in the Nationals. I was only young at the time, but I knew what my goal was, and I trained seven days a week to get there. Every day I would come home from school, have a quick snack, and my parents would take me to train. I never missed a day of training; I wanted to win gold and go to the European championships and I knew this meant I needed to be completely committed to judo. All of my hard work paid off and at age fifteen I won a gold medal. Now I needed to compete in qualifying events to be selected for the Europeans.

Making time for an activity you love is the most rewarding thing you can do in life. When you play a sport or engage in an activity you enjoy, you enter your own world. Sometimes, when I'm at home after a long day, it's hard to force myself to get up and train – life can be so busy and packed with different things we need to do, and we can forget to devote time to the things which keep us happy and fulfilled. Staying active is hard, but the hardest part is getting up out of your house and starting. Whether it's painting, tennis, judo, rugby, or dancing, once you start concentrating on your hobby you will transcend into a new world and find a peaceful headspace. It's a form of meditation to embrace exactly what you are doing and focus on nothing else. So never be afraid to throw yourself into something you feel anxious about. When an opportunity arises for you, whether it's a 5,000 meter race or a poetry competition or a singing show, never turn it down out of fear.

Put yourself out there and try new things, because there's nothing better than the feeling of achievement when you succeed. The feeling of winning is overwhelming – it is recognition that you are the best in that moment. However, in sport things can change so quickly. If you give up training, even for a small amount of time, you can become nothing when you try and compete again. When I was competing for the British squad, there were other people in my category who were just as good as me and I knew if I took any time off my success could vanish. Even though at times it can be difficult and stressful for any sportsperson, I always try to train hard, try my best, and stay on top of my game.

My judo coach was another reason I trained all the time and stayed so committed to the sport. As I am a trainer now, I understand how much a coach can encourage their students to achieve victory. Ambition always burned inside of me, and my coach, Leigh Davis, was very strict and dedicated to helping all of his students. Leigh always made sure everyone could get to training sessions; some less privileged students had parents who worked in the evenings or couldn't drive, so Leigh would personally drive these students to and from training and competitions. He never treated his female students differently to his male students – he saw us all as equal athletes and never made anyone feel any lesser because of their gender, instead he just focused on what we could achieve. Leigh removed any barriers which could prevent his students from training, and he instilled self-confidence, meaning we could all train and succeed.

After winning gold in the Nationals, I wanted to compete in the European Championships. Qualifying competitions were held all year round and they took place over many countries in Europe. I had an opportunity to travel to Belgium, France and Holland. However, in my final qualifying competition, I dislocated my elbow. I tried to use a judo move in which you put one of your elbows underneath your competitor and push them up as hard as you can, but the girl I was competing with pulled my arm back and I felt a surge of sharp, shooting pain. I fell to my knees screaming in agony. I looked across at my coach and he told me to get up. The medic checked me, and we started fighting again. Unfortunately, I felt the same pain again in my arm and the medic had to check me again. Now I knew this was my final chance at getting selected for the Europeans, because once the medic comes on to the mat three times you're no longer allowed to fight. I made the decision to carry on and, using only my good arm, I managed to throw my opponent and win the fight one-handed. Afterwards, my arm had begun to swell up severely and I was in a lot of pain, but I couldn't rest for long because my next fight was the final, which took place less than an hour later. When it came to the match, I didn't put up that much of a fight, as I didn't want to make my injury worse, and I let my competitor win as my arm still throbbed with pain. I won silver in the competition and managed to qualify for the European Championships.

While I won my place in the European Championships, I was also working towards sitting my GCSEs in school and my parents were getting a divorce. Training for judo became a way for me to separate myself from the stressful things going on in my life and just have time to focus on myself. It allowed me to have a headspace where I wasn't thinking about my parents separating. I spent a lot of time building strength in my arm and participating in training which would keep me active without making my arm worse. As summer came and I finished my exams, my arm still wasn't fully recovered but with all my efforts I was able to make it to Hungary for the European Championships of 2002 where I competed. After everything that had happened, perhaps some people would want the summer off, but I felt I couldn't throw away such a huge opportunity.

I won over 300 medals and trophies for judo by the time I was seventeen. Then, when I was eighteen, I went to the University of Loughborough to study Sport and Exercise and Science. Judo began to fizzle out of my life because not many other people at Loughborough were as experienced as I was, so I didn't have many people to train with. At the same time, I struggled with how difficult university studies were, and during my second year as a student I decided to drop out because being there didn't feel like the right choice for me at the time. After some time in England, trying to work out what I wanted to do, I decided to move to Spain to be with my mum who had lived there since her divorce. She was running her own restaurant business' near Alicante. I started working in restaurant jobs myself, and four years passed as I moved between different jobs as a waitress. While I truly enjoyed living in Spain, eventually the time came where I had to make a decision about what I wanted to do with my life. I hadn't been practicing judo as much since I quit university, but I knew how much I enjoyed staying active and wanted to work in a role where I could help people. I decided that the right path was to become a personal trainer. After taking a six-week intensive course, I qualified and decided to move back to England so I could gain more clients. I took different administrative jobs while also working as a personal trainer part-time.

MMA fighting started to be introduced into my life as I began going to the gym more frequently and training for my own personal growth. My coach, strongly encouraged me to start MMA training and so I began taking more of his classes and he taught me to kickbox, to wrestle and how to combine all the different martial arts required to be a mixed martial artist. Ronda Rousey, the first female fighter to get into the Ultimate Fighting Championship (UFC), an undefeated MMA fighter, was rising at around this time, and I was in awe whenever I watched her fights. She also had a background in judo, she had been an Olympic judo fighter, and I found this very inspiring. After many years without competing, I decided to enter an MMA and a K-1 Kickboxing competition in 2013 – I won gold in both. Once again, hard work and training meant I could prove my strength. These successes and my first cage fight against Molly McCann meant I was getting a lot of offers for more fights and I knew it was time to make a major decision in my life: I quit my administrative job and committed full time to my training. For five or six days of the week, I would leave the house at nine in the morning and come home at nine in the evening. I won my second MMA fight at the end of 2014, against Wendy McKenna, another amazing fighter, and together we also won Fight of the Night – we were the only females competing that night, so it felt extremely empowering to be recognised as strong and entertaining fighters.

As I became more serious about MMA training, I met my husband. He was very supportive and attentive and was intrigued by my martial arts background, unlike other men I had dated who were jealous of how much of a contact sport judo and MMA can be and the close proximity with the guys I trained with. But my husband always lets me do what I want to and encourages me to be happy. Within a year of meeting, we both knew we wanted the same things and we got married.

Unfortunately, shortly after my marriage, just as my MMA career began to flourish in 2015, I tore a ligament in my knee and wasn't able to compete. I had other fights offered to me which also fell through due to the show being cancelled and opponents pulling out. Then I became pregnant with my son, and my whole life changed. He's four years old now, and I take him to sports classes often; he does swimming, football, tennis, gymnastics, kickboxing and I look forward to when he's old enough to try judo. I know I could work full time and send him to nursery full time, but I want to have quality time with him while he's young. My advice to young mothers would be to involve your child in sports from a young age, it has endless physical and mental health benefits and I have found taking him to these classes is a lovely way for us to spend time together.

My parents always had faith in me; I strive to have that same faith in my son as he grows up. Sometimes he used to play with a doll – It doesn't bother me that this might be thought of as a toy for girls, all I want is for my son to be happy. I was a tomboy when I grew up, and now I don't even bat an eyelid if my son wants to push a pink pushchair around. He'll be whoever he wants to be, I can't stop that, and why would I? Society focuses so much on materialistic problems. There needs to be a shift in society's attitude; we should be getting out of the house and getting on with our own lives by doing the activities which make us happy. Instead of focusing on what others are wearing or doing, we need to focus on real, fulfilling hobbies and passions – I believe this is the best way to live an ambitious and creative life.

I still train in MMA sometimes, and I still feel like I'm 24 even though I'm 34 now. Whatever has changed in my life, I'm forever an adrenaline junkie and I love being adventurous. Whenever we have family events, I'll always be out playing football in the garden with my nephews. I don't feel my age; I'm full of energy. Although I used to feel guilty that I am no longer training every day, I have realised I need to let that go and just enjoy training. I am keeping my body strong and working hard, and this is enough to be proud of myself.

In my life now, I have started trying out different things and walking down different avenues. I want to make a difference in the world, and I know that teaching children martial arts, training people at the gym and helping people be more active is really impactful. At the gym, I help to advise some women who feel nervous and apprehensive about martial arts or strength training and watch them become better and/or stronger. I love knowing that I've been able to help these women to gain confidence and achieve new skills.

More recently, after my MMA coach retired and focused on power lifting, a sport where people perform three different lifts (squat, bench press and deadlift) - lifting various weights. During this time I wasn't able to focus so much on competing in MMA, which is when my coach persuaded me to try a powerlifting. This gave me a sense of purpose as I felt lost when not working towards an end result. I was surprised to learn that around 85 percent of the powerlifting team (called Barfight) at my gym were female! I began training for my first competition which was in December 2019, and my performance at this event meant that I qualified to represent Great Britain at the European championships. The competition has now been postponed and I have been training ever since the lockdown was lifted. My heaviest lifts that I have achieved so far is a 130kg deadlift and 100kg squat, which I am extremely proud of given the fact that when I had started Powerlifting, my personal best was 90kg deadlift and 65kg squat. I'm so excited to see where this takes me and how much heavier weights I will be able to lift.

The atmosphere during powerlifting competitions is electric- everyone is cheering each other on, even your competitors. I am so grateful to experience this energy and it is all down to my coach. His name is Jacek Toczydlowski (Jack) and he impacts so many diverse women and encourages them to be their best without any judgement and prejudice, removing cultural and societal stigmas surrounding power lifting. I'm forever grateful to have him by my side as a friend and coach. He has had a huge impact on my life and helped me to supersede my own expectations, in both MMA and powerlifting. He has always believed in me even when I did not believe in myself and I love what he is doing for women.

My advice to all women is to never stick to what society expects you to do. It's everyone's responsibility to encourage others to be the best they can be. I want every woman to recognise her infinite capabilities. All the women in the world are so strong, they just may not know it yet.

CHAPTER 4

Odds against Time

PANNA VEKARIA

Panna Vekaria, a woman of substance, has had an extraordinary life for those who know her well. Her vivaciousness and determination in breaking the taboos around being a single parent to her two children after having faced early menopause in her thirties is commendable. The trials and tribulations of Panna's life have shaped her to be an incredible daughter, sister, mother and person of integrity. Her passion for life and authenticity came across so colourfully, as she shared her story with me alongside her beautiful baby son.

*

My parents are from the Gujarati community, my father was born in the state of Gujarat whereas my mother was from South India. When Idi Amin, the President of Uganda in 1972, ousted Ugandan Asians (most of who were Indians), my grandfather chose to come to the UK, for life would've been so different if we had decided to go back to India. We have seen so much change in the last 42 years since I was born. We used to live in Wembley in northwest London, where many Indians from the Gujarati community live. It was very nice living with people around you, who you could play with, celebrate festivals with and enjoy the community spirit. I remember how we used to take presents to families and children during Diwali and Christmas.

We come from a small village called Madhapar in Gujarat. It is one of the largest villages, also known as a model village. It is always nice to go back to old places, which hold beautiful memories for me. My father took us back to Uganda and told us of the places he had visited, the school he studied in and the pranks they all used to play on one another. I remember the gleam in his eyes every time he spoke about it. He was a big influence on me; I was always besotted by the amount of information he had about everything. Growing up, girls always tend to idolise their fathers and I was no different.

During the UK recession of the early 1990s, my school was about to close its doors to education, and it was nearly impossible for me to find another one. All my friends went to Buckinghamshire, but I lived in London. They managed to get admissions to schools straightaway, but they couldn't slot me in. After much despair, my father found an all-girls residential school in Mussoorie, Uttarakhand, India. My sister Khyati and I travelled to India to study in this very strict and disciplined school. We were very athletic, and our housemistress always used to pamper us. We all had to get up early in the morning for morning physical education and then get ready for school after. The facilities at the school were very different to being back at home in England. Hot water was only available for an hour in the evening for the whole school, which meant that we had to rush our dinner and wait for our turn in a long line to eventually be able to have a hot shower if we were lucky. In the morning there was never any hot water and we literally had to splash cold water on our faces, put some face cream on and be ready for the day. The other alternative was to have a freezing cold shower in the morning which was unbearable. I can recall when there were times during National days and they would give us coloured rice, which would then get washed off to serve as white rice. I told my father to register a complaint, to at least get basic amenities for us and the other students, especially when we were paying them such high fees, but nothing seemed to change. However, I do now feel that those were my formative years and that has made me tough on the inside and paved my way to take on everything that life has thrown at me so far. If given an opportunity, I would love my children to experience boarding school life, but I wouldn't send them to India.

Since my youth, I wanted to join the army and my Dad was totally against it; he wanted me to study accountancy. Much to his despair, I ended up doing a degree in sports and exercise science because I had envisioned taking sports to developing countries and promoting it amongst disabled children, younger children and especially girls. I started reading up on a lot of history of these sports and realised there is so much background and knowledge about how they came about. I used to go to the British Library and did a lot of study on it and understood that there were many sports that India needed help with, there was so much I could offer.

I started working with the girls in the Asian community, making sure they would get a fair chance. It all started with organising a five-a-side football tournament for charity, which lasted for 4-5 years. Earlier our community never really thought about creating opportunities for girls in sports. Today, the chances are better but still quite low to what I think it should've been. It was understandable that in society when the boys get together and make a football team to play on a Friday. But it would look like a scene from Bend It Like Beckham to see a group of Asian girls trying to play football on any day. You do find women teams in cricket but it is hard to find girls playing for charity or any other purpose. All I ever wanted people to know is that if they are interested in playing sports and believe that they can take it up as a career, then one should.

My involvement with charities began when we set up our own Foundation after seeing my grandfather's work with a blind and disabled charity in Gujarat. In India, if a child is born disabled, the parents abandon them and refuse to take responsibility. Believe it or not, these children can be some of the brightest people you would ever meet. We wanted to do something for them and there were a lot of us who wanted to donate but back then you had to be in India to give that kind of money. So we set up the branch here, a UK asset foundation so people can come through us and then we can transfer the funds, as this created a clear pathway and there were no admin costs involved. As a trustee, we were always looking to get involved with different charities and today we have done a lot of work with Akshayapatra and Able Child Africa, who work for children especially in Uganda and Kenya.

I firmly believe in working for the cause of women. Although work has been done in bringing awareness to women related issues - physical and mental, somehow rural areas in India continue to follow the old ways of working, especially when matters of menstruation are concerned. However, in India, there are a lot of ashrams for widows but maybe we need to focus on them here in the UK. I have seen it with my mother: she was someone who was so active around the house and in business, but completely gave up after my father passed away. I feel that my mother has lost all motivation to be out and about and do all that she used to before. She doesn't have a social circle anymore and I feel there are many other women like her who have lost the desire to live their life to the fullest. I want to do something for them so they keep themselves alive for their families.

My father passed away suddenly in 2013 in Ahmedabad, India. I remember it well, along with my sister and mother. We were in London when we received the news of my father being unwell. I decided to leave straight away with my uncle and cousin and somehow had a funny feeling that they were all hiding something from us. By the time I reached the airport, I started getting text messages saying, "Panna, I am really sorry about your Dad". That very minute someone called and started crying on the phone and I knew we had lost our Dad. That was the longest flight I ever took, and I was restless, waiting desperately to get off that plane. Once I reached Ahmedabad, a group of men came to receive us and I heard someone say: "Let us go to the hospital, and let someone take Panna home." I was furious and did not let them make their own rules, how dare they! I was his daughter and I hadn't flown down all this way to be shunned out of all the important decisions. I went to the morgue to see my father one last time and I knew I would have to step up and take over for the family. All arrangements were made, and my family flew down too. I had to toughen up and abide by the rules I had set. I made sure my father's body was taken to his village for ceremonies in a proper ambulance and not a boxy van that the others had organised for his funeral. I told them that there would be no tea breaks in the middle of the journey. This was important as when the ambulance switches off, the cooling turns off. I could hear people say: "These girls are difficult to deal with", but I would not let any other take advantage of the situation only because we were girls.

Before my father passed away, he always used to tell me how he wanted to be a grandfather. For that, I need a man, which meant I had to get married. But after meeting and being introduced to random men, who were just not to my liking, I realised that I wanted to be around for my parents and marriage was not something that needed urgent attention. However, my biological clock was ticking, and I wasn't getting any younger. It was in my late thirties when I was diagnosed with early menopause. I had the flu and really bad hot flushes coupled with funny moods. For two years I lived my life in this agony, and it wasn't getting any better. I started to do my own research to freeze my eggs and after sharing this with my supportive father, we agreed that I would start the process. I was always in touch with my father and kept him in the loop and he agreed to support me in this process, as long as he gets to become a grandfather. Normally, it's weird for a daughter to talk to her father about these things, but my relationship was very different. He used to call me up when he knew I had a blood test. He would ask, "What were the results like, what is the update?" It was nice to know that he was there backing me up.

That has made me really strong. After I decided to go ahead with the treatment, only one person questioned: "Oh, but what about the community?" We have been heavily involved with the both Hindu and Kutch communities. But I have always felt that I was doing nothing wrong by having a sperm donor and IVF. People will talk regardless; at least I discussed everything with my family, unlike most people who indulge in other activities behind their family's back. For me, if someone wanted to have a relationship with me, then I come with all of this attached. If not, I don't bother as I don't need that kind of negativity to make a decision that my parents are supporting me for. If I want something, I really make sure I do it.

I went to Spain for my treatment. A specialist clinic was recommended by a friend and they gave a great service, much better than in London. I was really impressed with how in a day I had my blood test, saw the experts at the clinic and how nicely they followed up through emails, even telling me when I was meant to start my medication and when to stop it or increase the dose. I was taking medication to thicken my endometrium, before they could attach the eggs to it. Luckily the sperm donor of both my children is the same and therefore they are biological siblings. I felt this was amazing as there are so many women out there who cannot conceive or do not want to compromise on their career and yet want children.

My first child, my daughter was born in March 2017. My father had already passed away by then. Before her, I had had two miscarriages and one ectopic pregnancy. I felt like the whole process was quite rushed. Even though I had warned the clinic of my early menopause, which they knew at the time and they attempted to restore my confidence, by making me buy almost £3000 worth of medicines on the Friday and the following Monday the doctor started telling me how this would not work on me due to my menopause. I went to another clinic, which seemed to work but only resulted in a miscarriage. It was awful. I remember I was in my very early stages of pregnancy and I had to be at an Army Diversity seminar in Brize Norton, a village in England. At that time the area had no phone signals or WiFi. I started with a stomach-ache at night which was said to be normal at the early stages of pregnancy. However, next morning I was bleeding profusely, and I knew I was having a miscarriage. Somehow, I managed to reach my cousin who lived nearby, and she called the clinic and informed them what I was going through. I packed a whole lot of toilet paper and drove myself to Grantham Hospital. The nurses there tended to me, cleaned me up and referred me to Lincolnshire Hospital where I was taken in an ambulance.

My sister picked up my car from the hospital and stayed with me. After we finished with the process, I told my sister: "You know, I can't do it. I have had a miscarriage and I am going to man up and accept it. Let's go for a drink, I just need a cocktail." The second time round, I knew what the feeling was and I called in sick and dealt with it the whole day on my own. After having a planned lunch at Baker Street in London, I went in for my scan. The lady who usually did my scan was unusually quiet and I could sense that something was not right. They told me to go to UCL immediately and go through the Accident and Emergency department. I was having an ectopic pregnancy. We went through it all and it took a long time. But surprisingly, no one told me about what happens next, or what was I supposed to do, or how I was meant to follow it up. It took a toll on me both physically and emotionally and I stayed with my mum for a couple of weeks. Friends kept pouring in and I decided that things happen for a reason and I just had to 'man up'.

My family has been my biggest source of strength. Yes, it would be brilliant if I had a man in my life but I have managed two years with my eldest daughter and now I have a son too. I do have my ups and downs but my mother's side of family are always around to help. They would say: "When would you like us to babysit?" or I can just call my sister and say: "Can you take over this weekend so I can sleep?" We work really well together and that is very motivating. In fact when I told my mother I was having another child, she was so happy and she said: "That is great! At least they both will have each other." Strangely enough my daughter recognises my dad even though she was born after he passed away.

When she started talking, she would point at his picture and say, 'Dada', and now every morning she goes to the prayer room and gives him a flying kiss and comes back.

I have always tried to 'man up' whenever I felt sad. I inherited this attitude when I served in the Army Reserve. It was difficult to take that up being a woman and from an Indian background. However, I am glad I did. I was a soldier under training and even though I was not a qualified one, I still got to do the Cenotaph march with my unit at Whitehall. There was a lot of training to go through, learning how to march, how to hold a weapon whilst marching. It was all worth it. I remember when my whole family came to see me do it.

I was in the Army Reserve for three years, from 2011 to 2014. You know when they say Army is your family, they truly are. I made friends, learnt how to hold my drink, learnt so much about discipline and things that we as civilians do not think about. You have your own banter and they all have your back. We have crawled in the mud, been physically fit and have understood the importance of a weapon. One has to be a strong being to be able to endure the harshness that comes with it. You would have corporals shouting at you, sometimes one would question why they can't talk normally. But it made me a whole lot firmer and I think it made me get ready for the world. As a fun part of it, I got to do cliff diving, which I probably wouldn't have done on my own. It was an experience I can never describe and it helped get rid of the fear I had of adventurous activities.

Professionally, I used to be a General Manager. I studied Sports and Exercise Science but I couldn't find a job in that field. Instead I joined Vascroft, my father's company. I have worked in various departments, from accounting to health & safety. I was looking after the vehicle fleet and general management of the company. But when I came back after having my first baby, they made me an assistant buyer, which meant buying material and I really enjoyed doing that. I have a line manager who guides me about what is right and what is not. I don't mind working under someone, as long as I get to learn something that I like, especially when I can go to someone at any point of the day if I don't understand a certain aspect, for example the difference between sharp sand and soft sand. I get along with all my fellow employees, even the team on site, who I respect as they keep the business growing. The whole workforce acts as a team and as a family.

As a person, I have always strived to use the determination and the fire that I have in me. We can do so much, we can talk about so much and yet people try and hush up major topics of discussion these days. Since my father's death, I have calmed down a whole lot. Earlier I used to say what I felt to people's faces. If I didn't like something, I would say it. But with time, priorities change and I feel I am in a better place. If you ask me for advice, the only thing I can tell women aspiring to become mothers is that something will have to give. Parenting is not about having a child and giving them to the nanny to raise. It is hard work and you need to be solely responsible for it. If you have an active social life, maybe you need to think again before deciding to become a parent. Keep your family together because there will be no one else who'll stand beside you in times of need. And be yourself, only that will take you to where you want to be.

CHAPTER 5

Flying High

DR YOGE PATEL

Yoge recently won the Asian Women of Achievement/Women of the Future entrepreneur award in 2019. This was the first time that I discovered her phenomenal achievements. She has been nominated for a 2019 Women in Defence UK Innovation Award and she is included in the Top 100 Asian Stars in Tech List - a prestigious showcase for the diversity and vibrancy of the tech sector in the

UK. Her career started with a Research Fellowship at Shrivenham College, Cranfield University, a PhD in Flight Control from York University and a healthy appetite to change the technology status quo. She spent 10 years at the former Government Laboratory, QinetiQ, leaving as a Fellow in Flight Systems with a track record in delivering innovations with multi-disciplinary teams. She is the Chief Executive Officer of the Blue Bear Group and an authoritative and respected figure in the Aerospace and Maritime Industry. Her calm manner and straight forward character is a reflection of the humble upbringing she had in Mombasa, Kenya. I was fascinated by her journey in the exciting and competitive world of Artificial Intelligence.

*

When I stepped off the plane in Gujarat, I felt the warm breeze embrace my entire body, with the distinct smells and sounds, I arrived to a place that was once my home for a short time. I left India in 1966 with my mother and three siblings in tow on a ship to join my father and rest of the family in England. It was a long, arduous journey, almost two weeks, heading to an unknown land almost as mysterious as my birthplace in Mombasa, Kenya. I was a tiny two-year-old when my parents decided to leave Mombasa for India. They were true entrepreneurs and risk takers, fearlessly relocating over three continents with our large family of nine.

Growing up in the UK came with its challenges, but my memories are distinctly positive. My parents were the source of this: a pragmatic father and empathetic mother who made everyone's dreams come true. When I was fifteen, I remember observing my dad taking my brother along with him to do car repairs and I would wonder and challenge my mum about this. "Why is dad always taking my brother? Why can't I go along?" I would ask. I was always a bit of a tomboy. It wasn't until I was twenty-one and having passed my driving test, my parents surprised me with a birthday gift - my own car! My dad had fitted it with a new engine and shortly after, he invited me to change the clutch on my car. It was the best two days that I'd spent with my dad on DIY, crawling around the car having read the manuals and discovering the various parts and understanding how they all functioned. In those times, this would have been perceived as something that fathers only did with their sons. I was forever curious and thankfully my parents' progressive thinking helped me to achieve results in science, technology, engineering and maths.

I encourage other parents to not segregate your children and let them have equal access and opportunity in everything, removing all barriers. Let the girls of your family think about engineering, coding and all those geeky things and let the boys think about creative vocations such as a chef or musician or artist. Doctors, lawyers or accountants are not the only respected professions in the world.

Whilst my parents were busy keeping us fed and watered, there was always an emphasis on strong educational ethics, in common with most Asian parents. When we were young, my father used to come home from work and we'd all sit down and scrawl the alphabet and do our sums. There wasn't any firm guidance in terms of what we should or shouldn't do, we were simply expected to apply ourselves and do our best. When I chose engineering, I didn't have any: "Oh, engineering, surely not?" I was fortunate not to have any resistance. I used my engineering degree to design avionics and software for the aerospace industry before running my own company in the same sector. Two of my sisters knew they wanted to be lawyers so they followed their dream to study law. My other sisters and brother are doing exceptionally well in their chosen fields too – notably in education and finance.

I have applied my family values throughout my entire career. My collaborative approach to life in general has undoubtedly been influenced by my parents' values. I have been able to use these values to navigate my life through complex landscapes, always thinking about the collective rather than the individual. My parents have demonstrated simple but effective principles for as long as I can remember and, through perseverance and collaboration, have travelled great distances and thrived in spite of the social and economic difficulties they faced. Moreover, they have actively harmonised their children's lives within the wider society. This is a real strength as some of my siblings and I have married out of our community at a time when it was a taboo.

Over time, my parents simply embraced mixed cultures in their desire to support us. I am able to pass these values on to my two children, Katie and Sam. I met their father Simon while I was studying for my PhD. I said: "Mum, I've known Simon for just over... well, quite a few years," and she said: "Well, you'd better bring him home then, hadn't you?" My parents welcomed Simon into the family. We were married and have two wonderful children, whose lives are enriched as a result of enjoying both cultures - Gujarati and British. A multi-cultural outlook is one of the greatest gifts that one can give one's children.

I've watched my siblings go through different types of marriages. My eldest sister and younger brother both had arranged marriages. Three of my sisters opted to choose their own partners, so called 'love marriages'. Back then that was a shock in our community! Mixed marriages were a taboo. When it was my turn, being the middle child, it was somewhat easier as my older siblings had already paved the way. There were instances where my mum would say: "Oh, there's a lovely chap, a doctor from XYZ , I'm sure you'd like him if you met him." I just replied, "Mum, please don't ask me to see anybody. I will tell you when I'm ready and then we can look." The reality was that my mum didn't get me to see anybody. And then one day I went home and said: "I think I might want to get married." And she said: "Oh, well, I'm sure I'll need to find somebody for you." She said this with a twinkle in her eye, knowing jolly well that I'd already found my own partner.

With all the mixed marriages in our family my parents have ended up being pragmatic advisors for friends and family on mixed marriages. Over cups of teas, they will readily share their wisdom. “Well, you know, they’re your children. You may consider supporting their wishes because they are most likely to do it anyway.” My parents were not always totally aligned in this thinking but have, despite their anguish, always supported their children’s wishes over time.

The manner in which my parents conquered their challenges gave me strength to face my own challenges. I was able to get through my divorce whilst coping with a tumultuous time at work. My values underpin my professional life too. They certainly came into play when, after returning from two maternity leaves, I had to deal with an organisation that had significantly reformed and rivalry among the new management; I was disheartened to see how a lot of what I had established and the capability that was invested in my team had been disbanded. My founding values and vision were now no longer applicable in this new environment. New management practice was deployed with an ethos and mindset that focused on financial gain above anything else. I really did feel that the organization had forgotten that people make businesses successful not just the corporate infrastructure. I eventually left work as a very stressed individual and took time off to recover from what was a roller-coaster ride of 3-4 years of trying to come to terms with the changes. This departure initially had quite a big impact on my health, but in the longer term I recognised that this single event was one of the biggest turning point in my life, that led to a much healthier, and importantly wiser, work-life balance.

The departure taught me a great lesson in life about how I had been judging people on my values only. Retrospectively, I realized that you have to judge people based on their values, not just yours, and genuinely respect different values. I started to read about the different types of personalities through books on the topic. This is where I came across Jungian psychology and transactional analysis. In today's professional world, when you undertake psychometric tests, they are, often, based upon principles of Jungian psychology. This type of behavioural analysis is great for anyone who wants a deeper understanding of themselves and is willing to make a commitment to changing their outlook. This was a transformative era of my life and one of my first reads, recommended by a friend, was a fantastic book called 'Games People Play.' It's by Eric Berne who writes about how people play games, often unwittingly, in everyday life and it describes both functional and dysfunctional social interactions.

In a nutshell, leaving work helped me to understand people better and to re-define a stronger me that could articulate my values, how they manifested in my everyday life and why they mattered.

Around 2006 it was time for a new venture, and this is when I joined Blue Bear, a small company renowned for world class innovation in unmanned systems and autonomy, as a consultant. Blue Bear was set up by a great man called Dr Phil Smith, who started the business in 1999 with a vision for producing, building and testing unmanned and autonomous air vehicles. We had worked together before and between us we had started many of the drone programs in the UK. Phil was a well-respected and charming individual but, like many visionaries, his forte was not managing people. He invited me in to help deliver technical work and manage people. With two young children, I initially didn't want to commit too many hours to work as I had already achieved what I wanted in my former career but was happy to help out where needed.

A core part of my strength is coming up with ideas for innovation, building teams, writing proposals, securing funds and then delivering against that. So, it wasn't long before Phil offered me the position of Managing Director. Again, I did not really want this position as it was not on my plan but did eventually take on the role and in due course bought out Phil so that he could enjoy his retirement. It was a scary decision at the time, but I can say that being Chief Executive of my own company has been an incredibly rewarding journey for me.

Serendipitously, it has also been a great platform for presenting a role model for women in defense. I am not naturally someone who enjoys the center stage, but I certainly have views that I feel could benefit the work community I serve and I am not shy about standing firm on these views. I suspect it is this firm stance that has led to my invitations to committees on UK strategy and policy forming. I tend to sit on two national committees per year together with University boards.

I also suspect that there are a lot of south Asians who, like me, do not like the publicity, but actually we can do a lot of good by coming out of the shadows and leading the way. I feel very honored that I am in the privileged position of being nominated for awards that give recognition to me, a Gujarati at heart.

My journey is a journey that has had subtle waypoints provided by many people and incidents.

Many people come into your life to shape and influence it. I can recall my uncle Ramesh Mamma's wise words where he would tap me on my shoulder and say: "Go and do a Master's degree as well, a Master's in Aerospace." I ended up doing a PhD in Aerospace. I have also been greatly influenced by so much of what I have read. One book that I recommend is called 'Johnson Livingstone Seagull,' by Richard Bach. He writes: "Argue for your limitations and they shall be yours." When somebody puts a constraint around you, test those constraints and challenge them and redefine them so that they work for you. "Listen to your conscience. It is a measure of your honesty with yourself." So, use yourself as the guideline of what's right and wrong. Those two phrases have stood me in good stead; when times are tough I always go back and say: "Okay, what's real and what's honest and let's deal with that."

I'm hoping our next generation doesn't throw away what has taken centuries to build in the Asian culture, which is respect and loyal understanding of where you belong. Importantly, we are a culture that constantly seeks to build a better future, sometimes at great cost to ourselves. There is a great poem, written circa 1900, that reminds me of this aspect of our way of being. It is by R L Sharpe and it is called 'A Bag of Tools'.

It's the second paragraph that really inspires me –

"Each is given a list of rules;

a shapeless mass; a bag of tools.

And each must fashion, ere life is flown,

A stumbling block, or a Stepping-Stone."

This poem is really about the choices and decisions we make in our everyday life as we create our future. In my world every single day counts in forging this future.

CHAPTER 6

Flow like a River

SHIVALI BHAMMER

Shivali Bhammer is a British born singer, writer, public speaker and actress. She was born in London, and having studied Economics & Philosophy, embarked on a career in investment banking, sales and trading at Goldman Sachs but quickly left to pursue her artistic passions. She was signed to Sony Music BMG and has released two devotional albums, The Bhajan Project and Urban

Temple which reached number 1 on the iTunes World Chart. Shivali was nominated for two Global Indian Academy Music Awards at the age of 23 and was listed in the Top 25 South Asian Artists under the age of 25 in England.

Shivali holds a diploma in acting, Kathak (classical Indian dance) and ballet. As a writer she has been published in newspapers such as The Financial Times, The Orange County Register, Science & Spirituality, Spirituality & Health, Hinduism Today, Spiritual Directors International and India Link on topics of philosophy and faith. Shivali is also an award-winning playwright, founder of A Conscious Stream Productions and a frequent public speaker on Vedanta, Karma Yoga, Jyana Yoga and Bhakti Yoga.

I interviewed Shavali on Zoom as she was based in the US at the time. During this turbulent time with Covid-19, I was fortunate to be able to connect with her, gaining her perspective of life in the fast lane and hear stories of wisdom and resilience. These insights were strengthened by her spiritualty and gracefulness.

*

Entrepreneurial spirit runs in my blood, from both sides of my family, and I am proud to celebrate this family trait. My mum was born in Uganda and moved to England at eight years old; at the age of twenty-one she bought her first property, and by the time she was twenty-six, she had seven or eight properties all within central London. She always wanted to be successful and entrepreneurial, and she worked exceptionally hard to achieve that goal. She's my most inspirational role model. My father, too, worked very hard and possesses a similar entrepreneurial spirit. He belongs to a reputable family in Gujarat, from the city of Rajkot, and when he was twenty-four, after studying at university in Bombay, he broke away from his family's successful business to run a restaurant - the second restaurant ever in Rajkot, named The Lord's Banquet. It is now one of the oldest and most iconic restaurants in the city. People visit from all around the world; it is top of the list, even Gujaratis themselves, when they are in Rajkot.

When my parents got married, my father left Rajkot entirely as my mum wanted to return to England. My parents moved to London and worked on my mum's business. Very few people are aware of my association with The Lord's Banquet, even though it's still running back in Rajkot. I'm essentially a Central London baby; I grew up in Bayswater, and I had a very happy childhood. I remember going to Hyde park with my great grandmother to feed the ducks, and I remember how, on special occasions, my father would take me to Pizza Express in Bayswater. These are rich, warm, irreplaceable memories.

It was a happy childhood, but it was not without hardship. When I was a child and my mum was visiting family in India, she was travelling in the backseat of a taxi on the motorway when the door of the car opened, and she went flying off into the road. She was left there; the driver just drove away. Luckily, she was rescued by people who saw her lying on the motorway - but she was in a coma, and the doctors thought she wouldn't make it. I was too young to really understand the impact of this accident, but I know there was a lot of pressure on our family at the time because my mum had lost her own mum when she was two years old. My grandmother had died in a car too, not from a car accident but from a brain haemorrhage, and this awful pattern put extra strain on our family.

My mum was in a coma for some months, and I remember that by the time she pulled through, her business was in distress back in London because nobody had been able to take care of the payments or manage the properties, as my father was with her in India. I stayed with my grandparents while she was in hospital, and I can recall how she looked when she returned home to London; she couldn't walk, she couldn't eat, and she couldn't speak. Losing my mum is probably the biggest fear I have now. I didn't lose her but seeing her like this made it a reality that I could have lost her. It's always kind of in the back of my mind.

Only two years after my mum's accident, my parents got divorced. I think people in our community don't necessarily talk about the implications of divorce, and as an Indian child you certainly never spoke about being unhappy. Whatever emotional turmoil that I may have experienced just wasn't a topic for discussion. Eventually, my mum and I moved from central London to Hampstead, to a block of flats where my mum's cousin and his wife lived. He became like a father to me, teaching me maths, attending parents' evenings with my mum, being there for my university graduation. We were very close.

I know I am very lucky that I come from that all-encompassing Gujarati family where everyone took such great care of me. Even though my parents were divorced, there were many people in my family who helped my mother raise me. Of course, I also had my mum, my idol, to look up to at all times. My mum is one of the most beautiful Indian women in the world. She has gorgeous long, black hair that is thick like a horse's tail and it trails all the way down her back. Coupled with her big oval eyes, she simply resembles a Bollywood film star. She's got this classic beauty and people look at her in awe of the way she is. But she isn't just beautiful, she's also a strong-willed businesswoman. While she was raising me, after her accident and recovery, she decided to start from scratch and began a nursing home business, and our lives changed forever.

My mum, as a single woman investing in nursing homes, created an incredibly successful business in the care home industry. Her company, Sunshine Ventures, was so accomplished that she ended up on a list of 50 top Asian businesspeople in the UK. When my mum bought her first nursing home, everybody told her she couldn't do it. I think that throughout her whole life, people always said no to her, and put limitations on their ideas about what she was capable of. This is why when she was raising me, she never put me down or said I could not do something. I come from such a strong mother, who enrolled me in the best schools in London and supported all aspects of my education and wellbeing. I am hugely grateful for this.

Most Indian children and most Indian women are taught two things in life: you must attempt to get good grades so you can get a stable job you can depend on, and you are taught that you should get married. If you can do all those things, then you have led a successful life. On the one hand, that's probably what was expected of me, but on the other hand, I come from a family who have taken risks. My mum never said no to me, and perhaps quite unlike any other Gujarati girl I have seen, I was encouraged to pursue the arts by her.

I grew up literally on a stage. I started practicing ballet when I was two, and I continued it for eighteen years. I went to acting school, I started singing, I played music from age fifteen. I was talented in the arts and my mum never stopped me, but I also sought an academic route. I grew up with this divide between the expected traditional route, and the risk-taking route my own parents had embarked upon themselves. Ideally in life, you are told to pick one, but I think it's really hard for Indian women because you are taught to play it safe. You're told to be a doctor, a dentist, or go into finance, not to become an actress or a singer or a dancer. But my mum had a different vision for me and enlisted me in arts.

When you do everything, you don't have a focus and you lose out on becoming the top of what you could be. I was stuck between two paths, and I always played it slightly more safe. Anything that I have achieved I think has been a blessing, opening doors for myself, allowing me to embrace the diversity of life, and become a holistic human being. When you have this huge range of experiences, you become somebody who can walk into a room and identify with every single person there. On some nights I can't sleep because I think I haven't done enough, I know I'm capable of more, I should be doing more. Or I think that I should get married, and settle down, that my clock is ticking on having children. I wonder, why as humans do, we feel that we need to be confined? Why do we feel that we are only here to experience a particular path, and everything else is a distraction? What is a distraction? Life is just time. It is a series of experiences, and it is for us to choose what each one means to us.

At first, I followed an academic path and after completing a degree in economics and philosophy, I started working at an investment bank. I remember sitting on the trading floor, trying to learn about volatility trading. Most people don't stay in banking long because you burn out; you've got a lot of money, but that's about it. I remember thinking I needed to consider what I really wanted. Fortunately, I wasn't pressured to make money because my mother had her business, so I had the choice. I think a lot of Indians may not have had this choice while they were growing up, to just sit and figure out what they wanted to do. But I did.

When I resigned from banking, I immediately began following my passion in the music industry: I went to Mumbai and was signed with Sony Music - I was the youngest person to ever be signed to a major Indian record label, and they had never signed anyone from the UK before. I was hungry for success. But I was also ready to learn some lessons; I had grown up with so much privilege and this was the moment, in Mumbai, when I stepped out of that life. I rented a room with two other women in Bandra in a small apartment, with nobody to help us. I led a very simple life: I would eat minimal food, I wouldn't spoil myself, and I solely focused on improving my singing. I stepped out of the world of banking and suddenly became an artist without much, but hearing my music on the radio, seeing it on television, seeing posters in shops, and my albums being sold at one of the most famous record stores in India, Rhythm House, it made it all worth it. It meant I was able to achieve everything independently.

I was young in the music industry, and there were a lot of restrictions about what I could do including what I could eat, what I could wear, where I could go, and who I could talk to. At the time, I didn't understand it, but now I do: they were trying to make me into a star. There were people who had been around for much longer than me and they were accustomed to how the industry worked, they knew what would be successful and what wouldn't. They recognised how to package me and my music in the right format so that I could add value. But I rebelled against it - I walked away from opportunities because I refused to let anyone tell me what to do. I regret some of this now because I have come to understand that in the music industry there are experts who know better than you, and they can guide you.

If you just listen, you can learn so much. I think that our generation of privileged kids are given so much confidence, that sometimes we think we know it all. But what we take for granted is that real life experiences give you something that formal education just can't. Your parents' experiences can never be replicated. But this doesn't mean that all of their advice is correct, and what younger people need to learn is to listen more. We tend to speak more and listen less. But everybody who walks into your life, professionally, personally, or even just for a moment, you can learn something from, if you listen and hear hard enough.

Sony Music was one of the best record labels in the world; they knew what they were doing, but I often refused to listen to them. Luckily, they convinced me to follow their advice and my album became one of the best known bhajan albums of the last decade. But I know that if I had listened that much more, and been more patient, I would be in a completely different place by now. But I didn't. Instead, I fell back onto the path I had so recently jumped off, by returning to London, taking a job in finance, and getting married. I was just trying to tick all the boxes; it was the biggest mistake I ever made.

I'm not okay with leading a life by just floating by meeting all of the traditional expectations. I have a hunger and drive for success and it is a must that I nourish this part of myself. However, before I recognised this, I slipped into the life of a housewife. I got engaged within four months of returning to London and married a man from a super wealthy family. I became spoilt beyond belief, I couldn't complain about anything. Except for the fact that something had died inside of me. I was a housewife; I left my job in finance because he was a trader and I was a broker and this was a conflict of interest. It was like I was a different person - I didn't even recognise myself. I think this happens to a lot of Indian women when you marry and suddenly don't know who you are. While I was in the marriage, I became very superficial, and I was more materialistic than I was artistic.

My husband and I were actually best friends before we got engaged, but it wasn't meant to be. I knew it wasn't, but I couldn't bring myself to break up the engagement. However, I was very lucky that I was married to an amazing person who I am still friends with today. We were married for a year when he told me he felt like I needed to be set free. That was exactly how I felt, like I needed freedom. I had signed up for something because I thought I was someone who I was not, who I could not be. I'm not the perfect Gujarati girl, whatever that is, who can live life as a housewife like that.

By the time I was divorced, I was still only twenty-six. My mum had been divorced so she knew what it was like and I learned quickly that you are treated differently once you are divorced. Some guys don't want you, they think you're ruined, and some women treat you differently because they think you're going to steal their husbands. The problem is, that even though it isn't true, you start to doubt your own self-worth. This was the first real test I had ever had in my life of doing something which was considered wrong by society. It broke my arrogance and made me question so many things about myself. I questioned every dimension of my personality.

I walked away from my ex-husband with nothing, and after seeing a media job opportunity in New York, I moved there to start working again. My family thought it would be too hard, that I wouldn't survive New York, but I wanted to do it and I worked my way up quickly in my new job. I could have stayed in London, but I wanted to experience something new, and I think living in a new country is a way to learn how to survive independently and have the chance to redefine yourself as a person. It's not easy to be out on your own without your family to rely on, but I think it is an experience which everybody needs to have, so they can learn things about themselves that they wouldn't have discovered otherwise.

The first year in New York was tough. One evening, after I had been in the city for two weeks, it was raining heavily and I was in such a bad mood. For some reason, I imagined my mum's cousin dying, the cousin who had been like a father to me, and I became very anxious imagining something happening to him - I talked myself out of it, reminding myself that he was fit as a fiddle, and he plays football, squash and tennis. But then I woke up in the morning to find out that he had died from a brain haemorrhage. My whole world just fell apart. There was something inside of me that couldn't register it because I had seen him and his wife as the perfect family, the family who didn't break. I was angry for a long time. I don't think I'll ever quite be over it, the grief struck me. I think you will always still be emotional about the death of someone who you love; it shows how alive the love is and how close someone can be to you even when they're gone. It's been six years since he died, and it's still painful because I still miss him.

Being a good human isn't just about getting everything right, it's about knowing how to grow when things go wrong. Humility and grace are powerful qualities which will help you to deal with the worst of times. There is nothing that will shake you to your core the way the death of a loved one will, and only if you experience it yourself do you understand what pain and loss is. When you understand that pain and loss, your love transforms; your love for others grows; your respect for time changes. You start to understand that you're not the controller of this world, and you just need to play your role as best you can.

If you define yourself simply by the way that other people are going to perceive you, you'll end up putting yourself in a negative position. Building strong principles and morals for yourself is absolutely vital. I worry for children who are now attaching themselves to what the outer world thinks, especially because of social media, but these displays you put online are all surface level. They aren't the reality of who you are. Getting your sense of self-worth from the outside can destroy your mind.

When I'm facing a problem, and I can't figure out what to do, I know I need to try and see the problem from a different perspective. I identify with it as a telescope effect - I'll zoom out from where I'm sitting at home and I see my problem, I see me, and I see the room, then I'll zoom out further and see the property, then the area where I am in London, then the UK, until I have zoomed so far that I can see the earth. Suddenly, I realise the vastness of what I am a part of. I've changed the lens on my mind, and my problem looks very different straight away. If I still can't get past a problem, I will try and find a source of moving water to help my thought processes flow. When you watch moving water, or you walk, or run, or dance, the movement represents change and flow, and a problem is like a rock in the way. But you're not the rock - you're the river, and the river continues to flow. Let yourself identify with the movement, and naturally that problem will release itself and it will start to flow along with your movement.

I lived in New York for five years, up until recently when I produced a successful play and brought it back home to London, where I am involved in the writing process. I'm now working on my next album with Sony Music of India. I've also returned to work in an investment bank; I am grateful to be able to balance everything which enables me to dedicate time to many facets of my artistic world. In the end, I haven't ended up needing to choose between one path, just to work out how to balance both of the paths which I want to pursue. I have always tried to dedicate myself to so many different projects at the same time, and it was at times strenuous - the difference now is that I am stable. I am rooted. When you are younger, you try to dedicate yourself to a hundred branches and you haven't even built the bulk of the tree. You have no roots underneath; you're trying to build the best part when there's nothing underneath yet. Now, I have the roots so no matter how many branches I have, it's fine because I can sustain and hold everything up.

CHAPTER 7

Oneness with the World

HANSA PANKHANIA

Hansa Pankhania is an author, consultant, trainer and coach, helping clients to become stress-free and successful. Her mission is to reach out to individuals and organisations and help people feel peaceful, relaxed and productive. Her approach starts with making very small changes in people's daily life. She is a Fellow of the International Stress Management Association and author of the trilogy ‘Stress to Success’. She is a hardworking, dedicated entrepreneur who set up her own consultancy firm after completing a degree, through which she researched stress management techniques.

During our interview, Hansa explained the crucial links between our mental and physical health and how important it is to understand our emotions and express the way we feel. As a writer, Hansa’s work is driven by a passion for helping others, sharing the knowledge she has gleaned. She is committed to improving children’s mental health through stress management books. And as a mother and grandmother who is concerned about the future of the world for her grandchildren, Hansa’s next writing project will discuss how people and the planet can live in harmony.

*

My parents raised me with strong humanitarian values, to care for everyone around me and to share our pain in order to help each other. Growing up as British subjects in Kenya with Gujarati Indian heritage, my siblings and I share an honest, open connection and our family radiates unconditional love, with no strings attached. My brothers are heavily involved in voluntary work, and I too wish to dedicate my life to helping others – I am the first in my family to take an entrepreneurial route, providing alternative ways for people to improve their wellbeing.

When I visited Deepak Chopra's wellness centre in California with my daughter in 2004, I became obsessed with the idea of setting up my own wellbeing hub. Deepak Chopra's centre was truly inspirational: he had meditation rooms, workshop rooms for self-improvement and connecting to your spiritual self, spa treatments, and yoga classes. The wide range of different types of wellbeing interventions felt like such a powerful idea to me, and I wanted to recreate it back home in England.

As a professional counsellor and consultant at the time, my vision was for a centre to have counselling and other services focusing on stress management and wellbeing. I didn't know anything about business when I set out to create my centre, but I was very determined, and so I began attending workshops about how to set up a limited company. This centre was something I believed would make a real difference to peoples' lives, and I taught myself what I needed to know in order to create it. After a lot of self-teaching and researching, I set up the AUM centre in 2005.

Staying at Deepak Chopra's centre encouraged me to become aware that when we are suffering from physical ailments, we need to fully consider our mental health. In order to recover, we must listen to and express our emotions. While at the centre, I learnt about Chakra meditation – I learnt how different emotions are connected to different parts of the body and how, for example, if you are suffering from health problems and your throat is hurting, this could mean your throat chakra is blocked and you may be suppressing your feelings. The irony is that, as an Indian woman, I was taught these Eastern concepts by friends who did not have Eastern heritages, but who had been practicing these ancient Eastern concepts for far longer than me. The visit to Deepak Chopra's centre made me realise that I wanted to tie together Western and Eastern approaches to health: in order to help my clients feel their best. I now combine my university research into Western stress management with the Eastern acknowledgement of the intrinsic links between our mental and physical wellbeing.

Opening a wellness centre was a risky move – I was warned by my accountant that it might not be viable and could result in losses. Initially, he was right, and shortly after setting up the centre a number of important events began happening in my personal life – my children were getting married, and my father-in-law became very ill – so I decided to split the centre in two and continue running a consultancy while the other half became a holistic therapies centre. AUM consultancy is still running today.

As the first entrepreneur in my family, I am proud that I have designed a consulting centre which can help people to manage their stress in the way which works best for them. Our centre offers a range of different stress and mental health management services, and no matter who I'm counselling my aim is to connect with everyone on a human level. Regardless of whether a person works in business, as an academic, or as a housewife, every person can face difficulties in their life – my services help people to drop their barriers, acknowledge their stress, and discover the techniques which allow them to live life to the full.

I decided to become a counsellor while I was studying psychology and personal development at university: it was here that I realised how essential it was for every individual to understand their own mind. As I was sitting in a university session where we discussed personal development, one member of the group spoke about the emotional pain she was feeling. I began to suggest solutions to her and provided her with different ways to solve the problem. My tutor said: “Hansa, stop – we need to listen to how she is feeling.” These words stopped me in my tracks; I realised I never listened to how I was feeling myself. Instead of focusing on fixing a problem, sometimes we need to step back and consider our emotions.

On my way home that night after the session, I couldn’t stop thinking about how I did not take the time to recognise the way I felt. When I was completing my degree at university, I was already a mother and wife – I met my husband in college and had decided to get married instead of going to university – and I had many, many responsibilities to take care of as well as a lot of anger which I’d bottled up inside of me. I had so much repressed anger as a result of my step mother-in-law, who was a very vindictive and jealous person who made my life very difficult.

Through my personal development studies at university, I learned to give myself permission to express my feelings and my anger – I made the connection between my anger and health problems I was experiencing. I realised that if I released this stress through discussing and acknowledging that it existed, then I could recover and heal from my negative feelings. The strength I have gained through this is the same strength I use to help my clients become more emotionally aware and work through the different feelings they may have.

Whenever I learn something that helps me or helps a client, I always think about how I can share this knowledge with people. I always want to pass on information which could help others. One of the most powerful ways to share this information is through writing. Once my consultancy centre was running, I decided to write a book to share the different techniques I used for encouraging people to relax and manage their stress. I have now published three books on stress management. In my work, I use both Eastern and Western philosophies to outline the ways to ensure the mind and body are connected together in synchrony. The more I learn about connecting your mind and body in everyday life and in, for example, yoga or meditation, the more I practice on myself – I believe I can connect with people through my own experiences and develop my understanding of peoples' emotions by developing my understanding of myself.

After my book trilogy on stress management was complete, I published my fourth book, 'Best Of Three Worlds', which is a memoir about my upbringing in Thika, Kenya. My childhood was spent playing by waterfalls, learning Gujarati and English at school from teachers originating from India, Africa, and England, and growing up in a cosmopolitan environment surrounded by different cultures. We moved to England when I was seventeen, and I first visited Gujarat in India when I was thirty-five – after nearly twenty years in England. This was a big shock to my senses: cows and other animals were on the streets, you had to bargain for everything, and I had some of the best food I've ever eaten in my life. I found it really exciting to see signage in Gujarati, as I know how to read and write in Gujarati but had never experienced a place where everything was written in that language. Now, I have taken my children both back to the place I was born in Thika, and to Gujarat to show them the place of their heritage.

In my memoir, I also write on how first and second-generation Indian women, and other Asian women, are conditioned to be dutiful. Outlining the repressive conditioning faced by some women allows me to show readers how they can become more comfortable with their own emotions and realise it is okay to feel angry and be assertive. Holding negative content inside you will affect your everyday life and health; in order to feel happy and free, we must express our feelings. In my work with clients and in my books, I demonstrate how this is possible in safe and constructive ways.

Adults are not the only people who suffer from mental health difficulties – I have written three books for children about managing their stress, because individuals are beginning to suffer from mental health issues from younger and younger ages. I believe that the current attitude and infrastructure in the government for helping children with mental health problems is not enough. Solutions are given to solve problems on a surface level but not to prevent the problems from occurring in the first place.

Trained professionals are needed to manage the root causes of difficulties faced by children. My books aim to provide techniques for children to express their emotions and learn methods of relaxation. I use imaginative stories and a character called Chakraji which guides the children. The earlier that children start becoming mindful, the easier it is for them to manage their mental health during difficult times. My granddaughter, for example, is five years old and when she gets angry I encourage her to express how she is feeling to me, or write down or draw what's made her angry and talk about it, or focus on breathing techniques so she feels calm again.

As a mother and grandmother, I worry about the future of the world for my children and grandchildren. The climate crisis becomes more and more daunting every day, and the waste we contaminate our world with is dangerously unsustainable. I am at present working on two more sequels to 'Best of Three Worlds' called 'Best of One World' and 'Best of All Worlds' where I aim to address, not just the issue of sustainability but also of how different creeds, cultures and religions can live in harmony with each other and with nature. Underpinned by Gandhian humanitarian values, it is all about respecting each other but also about loving and respecting our natural environment. Hopefully, I will succeed in pinning down some of the specifics in these two books. We need to be thinking about how we can implement changes to save our planet – this applies both to the individual and the corporate world. My books always aim to provide information which can help to transform peoples' lives – this new focus on sustainability and society takes a new direction from the individual transformations outlined in my previous books focusing on mental health and concentrates on the collective change which needs to happen in our world to make it the best place for all.

It is self-belief which allows me to achieve my goals and focus on the writing I want to share with the world. Self-belief allows me to guide people to feel more confident and listen to their bodies. If you have true intentions, if you want to make the world a better place, the inspiration will come to you once you allow positive energy to flow through you. When you stay in touch with who you are, you will know what is the right thing to do for you and, even more so, for others.

Life is all about balance. Building a happy life requires careful management of time and boundaries, and I check in regularly with myself and ensure that I do not neglect any parts of my life or feelings. Every morning, I begin my day with meditation and yoga – this allows me to listen to myself and to my body. This practice means I can focus on how I am truly feeling and constructively think about what is best for me and what I should be doing during the day.

My life is enriched by a variety of different things I enjoy – I have been singing in a Bollywood band for thirty years, I write, I travel often, I spend a lot of time with my family and friends, I practice yoga and meditate, and I make sure I go on plenty of walks to take care of myself and think about my goals. I want to share whatever I learn with the wider world – I plan on learning something new every day and passing on any information which helps me. Managing my time productively is what allows me to lead a fulfilling life, and I would encourage anyone to begin by prioritising time management in their quest for health and happiness.

The most important advice I would give to anyone is to take the time to stop and think about how they are feeling. Meditation is a powerful way to do this; when meditating, you can truly focus on your mind and your body. When you believe in yourself and make the conscious choice to put time into focusing on yourself and being at peace, you are giving yourself value and respect– this will allow you to productively move forward and strive towards the things you want to achieve for yourself and others.

I believe everyone is loved and held safely by the universe and has something to offer that will make this planet a better place. I urge everyone to find this within themselves and share it with the world.

CHAPTER 8

The Blue Sari

NISHMA GOSRANI OBE

Nishma Gosrani OBE is a partner at a leading strategy consulting firm in financial services. She has won several prestigious business awards, including Young Achiever of the Year, Asian Professional of the Year and Management Consultant of the Year, and has been listed as one of the Financial Times EmPower Top 35 Future Leaders.

She is frequently described as 'someone to watch' by business leaders and politicians alike.

Nishma is passionate about equality and inclusion in the workplace. She was invested with an OBE in Her Majesty's 2020 Honours List for her work pioneering Gender Pay Gap reporting, which led to changes in the Equality Act. She is also highly involved in the arts and is a board member for Tamasha, a theatre company which promotes talented artists into mainstream media. She was also appointed a Fellow of the Royal Society for Arts. During our interview, Nishma shared the journeys of the strong women in her family as well as her own, discussed the difficulties with being a working mother, and shared her advice for passionate young women who want to be successful in their field.

*

We change the world when we utilise our opportunities and stand tall as role models for future generations. I know how lucky I am for the opportunities my family have bestowed upon me. Their capacity for hard work, dedication and support has allowed me to thrive as a businesswoman in London. I am third generation Indian emigrant; my grandparents travelled from a village in Gujarat to Nairobi in the early 1900s, and my parents grew up in Nairobi and eventually moved to London when I was four years old. As a successful woman in my field, I have the ability to help ensure the progress of equality in the workplace, especially for Asian women, in the hope that the next generation will be able to thrive without any of the barriers that colour currently presents. I am passionate about diversity and inclusion and have founded various forums in the corporate world to encourage women to collaborate, network, and build relationships: my goal is to change the prospects of women in the financial services sector.

Each generation should strive to do better than the last – I am in my position because of the two generations of women who worked so hard before me, and I will work hard to help improve the position of the generation of women who will come after me. My story does not exist alone; my story exists only within the context of two intelligent, generous, caring women, my mother and my grandmother, who overcame so much in order to succeed and provide for their families. My grandmother and mother gave me the confidence and power to fight in the face of adversity.

When my family moved to Nairobi, they were amongst the first Indian families to settle in Kenya, meaning my grandmother arrived at eighteen years old in a land where nobody spoke her language or was used to Indian culture. On this new continent, my grandmother did everything she could to provide for her family, and her entrepreneurial spirit was unstoppable. She decided to make delicious pots of chutney, the texture of jam, as my mum used to describe it, and sold them on the markets in Nairobi. Chutney is originally from India, and the local African community loved the idea of something quite exotic for them. My grandmother's trade became so successful that thousands of pots were sold, and over time my family turned the idea into a great empire.

In Nairobi, my grandmother had eight children of her own, but she was the mother to everyone; as more families from Gujarat arrived, my grandmother would care for almost all of the children in the community. The family home had perhaps up to twenty bedrooms inside, and she would provide for everyone – she was an amazing cook, and nobody left the house without being fed properly. My grandmother was a beautiful woman, she was very petite and extremely beautiful with light hazel grey eyes, which were very striking. She was meticulous with her hair and her outfit choices – my mother and I have both inherited this from her. In our community, it's customary to wear light colours when you are widowed – my grandmother was widowed when she was very young and her clothing choices were attributed to the loss of her husband, and also the loss of two of her children. She wore the most pristine Swiss voile saris, made only from very pale blue and white fabrics, and she had beautiful cotton net embroidered blouses that she would wear under cardigans when she moved to England later in her life, which is how I remember her.

My grandmother had a powerful community spirit and cared for everyone – she was the first female president of the Oshwal community in Kenya, a community which brought together those who came from Gujarat and retained cultural values and traditions. It's important to understand, however, that such individual smaller communities were developed years after the initial settlement of Asians in East Africa – to begin with, the Asian community existed as a whole, together, because of complicated friction with the local African population in Kenya. There was a sentiment amongst the local African population that Asian people had settled in the community with a commercial spirit that took over their land and jobs. East African Asians, therefore, felt that as they had arrived together, they needed to stick together and work together as a community in order to survive in this new country. Gujarati people did not distinguish themselves as Indian, because they belonged to a community of Sikhs, Punjabis, Muslims, and Ismailis – they coexisted together as East African Asian neighbours, working together, and so it was not for many years that individual communities began to flourish. Over time, the desire to preserve cultural values originating in different Asian communities became stronger, and my grandmother was very driven to ensure that we maintained the cultural and community beliefs she had been raised with in Gujarat. These beliefs concern supporting those around you, caring for those in need, and living a life without harming others. My grandmother was a very powerful character who was well known in our Oshwal community, and she was recently honoured as the first female founding president for Oshwal in Nairobi.

Through unbelievably difficult circumstances, my grandmother possessed great inner strength to carry on. When my aunt and uncle's car overturned on the highway and they died on the spot, my grandmother took on full care of my cousins, who were nine and eleven at the time. The car crash was so sudden and shocking that it left a painful mark on our family, and my grandmother went into a mourning period which lasted for two years. Family events were kept in a solemn spirit to respect the loss of my aunt and uncle. In those days in Nairobi, people were cremated on an open fire, and my grandmother told me she took her daughter's body in her arms, and to prepare her for cremation, in her meticulous way, my grandmother took out each tiny fragment of glass that had embedded itself into her daughter's flesh before washing and dressing her before her cremation. I think she felt this was the last thing she could do that would respect and honour her daughter; she wanted to ensure she properly cared for her child one last time.

My grandmother was extraordinarily resilient and resourceful, and when the civil war broke out in Nairobi in the seventies, she moved to England at the same time as my parents did, and lived on the same street as us. Once again, she had to adjust to a new continent and a new way of life, this time when she was in her sixties. She was a real force of nature, and while she articulated herself in Gujarati most of the time, she learned enough English to get by and learnt how to use a telephone – an old, spiral telephone which you operated by turning the dial with your fingers – so that she could call all of us in our houses in England. My grandmother called our house every morning to speak to my mum; I never appreciated at the time how much effort it must have been for her to memorise all the numbers in our family and to dial them each day to check in on us. Now, reflecting on it, I wish I hadn't dismissed her kind act so quickly. It can be easy to take for granted small acts of kindness until they are gone.

We must appreciate what we have and tell those who support us how much we appreciate them, because we never know when things might suddenly change: the maternal, caring souls of my mother and grandmother, whose positive spirits were irrepressible throughout the worst of times, are still with me now, and encourage me to face any challenges with strength and confidence.

Compared to my grandmother, my mother was quite a reserved character – she was always the peacemaker in the family, and she found it very easy to be happy with her own surroundings. She was a structured, organised individual who kept the family and cultural principles close to her heart. She was vegan and never drank alcohol. My mother was a very graceful and elegant individual, and her ideals of how to present oneself are still ingrained in me now. She has instilled in me the ways to be a good host and ensure my house is pristinely kept. Her cooking was so incredible and beautifully presented that she could have easily been an accomplished chef in a top restaurant.

Even as my mother's health wavered and gradually worsened over the years, her spirit remained beautifully strong. At times, she would be bedridden in the house and have to use crutches to get around, but she loved to cook and it was her passion so she would find the strength to do it. She was always a spiritual woman; her family very much instilled in her a sense of spirituality, a belief in peace between humans, and of living a life without harming others. In her later years, my mother became even more spiritual and remained an extremely positive, generous person. She suffered from a chronic condition called erosive rheumatoid arthritis, which meant her muscles and bones and joints deteriorated very rapidly, but somehow her willpower never faded. In spite of her illness, she maintained the house in perfect order because that's what she wanted to do: we would frustrate her to no end if we deviated from her pristine standards for any reason, and this is something we all remember fondly about her. When she stopped being able to leave the house, we taught her how to use WhatsApp and Facebook to help her stay connected with the world and with her family, and she became very intimate and close to her family as her illness got worse. When I was thirty-six, she died with me by her side in hospital, surrounded by her close family. There is no getting away from the fact that her poor health greatly affected the quality of her life towards the end, but all I can do now is let her spirit and strength remain alive in my memories of her, and look back fondly on the beautiful times we shared together.

Elegance was my mother's essence; she taught me everything about fashion and I have inherited her love of clothes and design. When I was younger, we spent many weeks touring India and exploring the differences between 'saris' across different regions. There's something very special about India. It brings to mind a quote from Maya Angelou: "We are more alike, my friends, than we are unalike." So many different cultures, religions, and generations all live together, and the warmth and affection you receive when you arrive as a guest is like no other place in the world. My mother's knowledge was incredible; the amount she taught me about fabrics and style was not far from a degree qualification. She showed me how to identify a real sari, how you crease a sari together so you can see the different threads against each other, and how to collect the different elements of a sari. My mother herself liked the Badhanis from Gujarat and Kanjivaram silks from south India, and she always dressed with a grace and simplicity that was not dissimilar to my grandmother's pristine appearance.

My mother was a best friend and confidante, perhaps not the same as the strict Indian mother you may expect, and I used to tell her everything. If she thought something wasn't right, she would tell me in no uncertain terms how she felt. When I went to university and started to pick up leadership roles - for example, President of the Students' Union and President of the Indian Society - my mother was so proud and got so involved; she would have everybody home for dinner, all of my friends, all of my fellow committee members, and she would help out wherever it was necessary. I think perhaps since she didn't have formal education, it was almost a part of her life that she hadn't lived, and it was fantastic to be able to share my experience with her. If only she had joined me at Buckingham Palace to receive my OBE, a moment she would be very proud of.

Our whole family was very strongly connected to my mother. When she died, we travelled together as a family to Rishikesh, in the Himalayan foothills of India and released her ashes into the Ganges river. It was an incredible experience, a surreal day, and I think it gave us the ability to move on from losing her. We all need some form of closure when we lose someone we love, and I was lucky to find this closure with my family in what is the most sacred place for a Hindu. My husband Vish was by my side the whole time in what were some difficult months, and he was extremely supportive. Together, as a family, we let go of her soul.

Every time I've faced difficulties in my life, I have found that going to work allows me to feel a sense of normality. While my mother was unwell, I worked from home but I also made sure I went into the office, so that I wasn't completely disoriented from my usual rhythm in life. Once she passed away, I went back into the office within a couple of weeks. Everyone was very concerned and asked me if I was feeling okay or if I thought it was a good idea to be at work, but personally, for me it felt good to go back into the motions of my usual routine. As humans, we're not particularly good at dealing with uncertainty and this was my usual space, that was familiar and helped me grasp at reality again.

I have been dedicated to my work as a consultant in the financial services sector since I finished university. The job involves focusing on clients and cultivating strong, key relationships which have served me well in terms of generating income for the consultancies for which I have worked. I have been able to take my career to its height over the last seventeen years because of three important things crucial to a successful career in any sector: integrity, relationships and reputation. Firstly, make sure people trust you, because this is essential to success in business – being honest and transparent with those who I work with has been key to how I do business. Secondly, build strong, trusted relationships from the beginning of your career. I have got where I am today as a result of the relationships I built as a young graduate which serve me well today. Finally, I think people often don't realise just how small their individual industries are – therefore, reputation is of paramount importance and will withstand any external challenges we face. This was the case for me after the Financial crisis in 2008.

One of the biggest challenges of my career was becoming a working mother, because, as every working mother knows, it can be really hard not to feel guilty about spending time away from our children. I had never taken a large amount of time off before I took maternity leave to have my son, and it was a huge deal for me to step out of a promising career to have a baby and then step back into it again. Almost every woman I know in my workplace has faced these similar difficulties about feeling guilty for working when they have children – it's important to remember we're not alone, and that there is nothing wrong with wanting a successful career as well as a family. I have found that dedicated planning is one of the best ways to ease guilt and ensure you get the quality time you need with your children: I have certain hours of the week reserved for time with my son, and during these hours I put away all of my electronic devices and pay full attention to him. We can be so easily distracted by work even when we aren't at work, so the precious time you do have available to spend with your children, make sure you are truly focusing on them.

My husband and I had great difficulty conceiving a child after I too was diagnosed with Rheumatoid Arthritis in my early 30s – it was only after three years of tests and two unsuccessful attempts of IVF that I got pregnant with my son, Yuvi, when I was thirty-seven –

the love of my life! The process of testing fertility and eventually going through IVF is incredibly draining, and, again, one of the things which helped me through this rough time was the structure and distraction provided by my career. My husband and I really wanted to have a child, but all the sitting around and hoping in the world doesn't change anything – stress can have a huge negative impact on our bodies, and I personally think that having distractions allowed me to think more positively instead of waiting in nervous anticipation for results. While I was undergoing IVF treatment, I met a nutritionist who told me something that has really stuck with me: "I know what you're going through and it's obviously having an impact on your body and your life, but you can be a mother in lots of different ways, even if you were not to become pregnant." While I have been fortunate enough to have my son, I think this message is important to everyone: there are so many different ways we can be a mother in this world, and we can use our motherly instincts in so many areas, not just with our own child. Although, this is not uncommon in Asian families today – I still find that it's not openly spoken about and I wish it were, as I know that my story has helped others.

There is a huge amount of work to be done to help the world, which means there is a huge amount of potential to be a mother in various ways and use our strengths to push future generations forward. Great differences need to be made in business and the arts and sciences for women and, in particular, Asian women. I am passionately involved in encouraging women to undertake the careers they want and I'm very keen to ensure that people who deserve to be in a position at work are allowed to get the best out of their environment and that we continue to push for a meritocracy.

I also volunteer for a project concerned with diversity in arts and theatre – about eight years ago, I took the role of chairing the board at Tamasha Arts, which takes individuals from Asian backgrounds who are interested in theatre, media, or film, and promotes them through the mainstream in order to make sure they are entitled to roles and situations which perhaps wouldn't typically go their way. Tamasha Arts has funding from the National Arts Council in England, as well as other funding from private sponsors. More recently, I've been working for an organisation called City Hindus Network, a fantastic project which enables a network of individuals in the city to come together, meaning that when people are entering the workforce they have a stable network around them before they even start. Lately, and as my own son enters prep education I have taken the role of Governor at an Independent Girls School. Gaining an understanding of how some of the most important aspects of our society function in order to influence them to create sustainable change is something I am very passionate about.

I've been fortunate to have worked with Pinky Lilani and to have been shortlisted for awards for her Women of the Future programme, which focuses on Asian women of achievement. Pinky Lilani has been a trail blazer for helping Asian women be successful in this country, and has also advanced her agenda to South East Asia. I spent time with her on two delegations – one to Singapore and one to Mumbai, during which we looked globally at what individual women are doing in the charity sector, in theatre, in the corporate sector, and strategised ways to bring these women together – there is strength in numbers and helping ambitious women get in touch with each other will only allow their incredible, driven, determined work in their respective fields to become even more powerful. Like Pinky, I am very fortunate to have some incredible mentors in my life whose wisdom and many years of experience helps me navigate my own set of experiences. There is one woman who has been there since the early years of my career and that is Jean Sharp. One of the most incredible women I have met in my life whose professionalism and integrity shines through in all the conversations we have had – I am very fortunate.

For women who want to be successful, remember this: don't put boundaries on yourself, don't sit on the fence – be passionate. Go out and explore every opportunity that's open to you. I think the next generation has a new set of boundaries placed on them by social media and the unrealistic expectations that it's created – focusing too much on social media means wasting precious time that could be used to get outside and begin taking advantage of the opportunities that will shape the course of your life. Education is the most valuable tool we can ever be equipped with, and it is your choice to set up your own personal strategy of how you will use everything you have the opportunity to learn and move forward. Create your own strategy for success.

CHAPTER 9

Achievers Mindset

MINAL MEHTA

Minal Mehta is a recognised leader for driving diversity and inclusion. At IBM, where she works as a Managing Consultant, Minal is always looking for ways to create a welcoming atmosphere for all and to encourage youth from minority backgrounds to pursue the career they want – she was presented with an IBM award as a Global Champion for Diversity and Inclusion in 2017.

Minal's focus on inclusivity extends beyond her workplace: from the age of eighteen, she has been involved in music-related projects with the record label Shiva Soundsystem with the aim of promoting and providing a platform for underground and under-represented artists. Her dedication to mentoring young people and encouraging everyone to pursue their passions, regardless of their background, reminds us that we should all be afforded the same opportunities and celebrated for our differences, because, as Minal says, diversity amplifies creativity.

*

When I missed out on a place at university because my grades weren't high enough, I felt like a huge failure. However, the gap year I took to improve my results from ABB to 3 As turned out to be the best thing that could have possibly happened to me, because I had the time to focus on one of my biggest passions: music. Ever since I was a young girl in music classes at the Bharitya Vidya Bhavan- a worldwide renowned centre for the promotion of Indian arts, music and language, music has been a huge part of my life. When I was on my gap year, I made contact with Nerm, a producer and broadcaster who runs the record label Shiva Soundsystem, and I started work experience with him, which was a dream come true as an eighteen-year-old. Working with Nerm moulded my ideas about the power of music – Nerm and his record label was, and still is, very focused on challenging the perception of Asian culture in the UK across music, film, radio, and events. I worked with Nerm to assist with the development of six BAME (Black, Asian and Minority Ethnic) artists for a cinematically released feature film, and I ran music workshops for BAME youth. My year began filled with uncertainty, but it turned out to be a year filled with passion for something I loved, and it shaped the way I approach life today.

Taking a gap year gave me a huge confidence boost; without someone telling me what to do, I was forced to be more independent and go after what I wanted. I worked with Nerm at Shiva Soundsystem solely because I had the confidence to reach out to someone who was above my seniority and involved in an industry I was passionate about. I have found that when you are motivated and show that you have enthusiasm for something, people will be interested – they may even want to help you. If you take a back seat and expect doors to just open for you, they never will. To make the most of what you enjoy, it's crucial to work out who you need to talk to and what you could do to make your ambitions become reality. Losing my place at university made me far less afraid of rejection – it helped me to realise that in life, you will encounter disappointment, you will have people turn you down, but that is no reason to stop: if you are passionate about something, don't let fear of failure stop you.

Having the confidence to reach out to people in the music industry has led me down amazing paths which would never have been available for me otherwise. Nine years have passed since my gap year, and I have completed a degree from the University of Nottingham and now work for IBM, but in my free time I also still work with Nerm. At Shiva Soundsystem, we are currently developing a project which challenges the social representation of women in India through the creation of a progressive, mainstream brand. I want to help break through the stigma around female Indian artists exploring their creativity: in India, as almost everywhere else, industries are often male-focused, so we are targeting the women who aren't afforded the same opportunities. Our project aims to empower female talent in India and motivate them to step forward and achieve success in the music industry. Currently we are developing tech-driven talent searches, creating content, and providing platforms to find women who want to perform. We are seeking out under-served and under-represented female rappers from the regions of India - looking to the villages as well as the metropoles. "Gully Rap", a grass-roots form of Hip Hop, is a sensation in India at the moment, and we want to expand its focus across the gender divide. To help break through to audiences and encourage artists, well-known singers in India are tightly integrated in the projects. Raw and undiscovered artistry is just waiting for us; now is the time to give talented women the chance to come forward. I feel extremely proud to be involved with sharing the stories of these artists with others.

Most recently, I have started working with Soumik Datta - a London-based Sarod musician, who captured my interest with his artistry and creativity. His latest album, 'Jangal', fuses Latin American and Indian instruments to create sounds to reflect the global climate change crisis and deforestation challenges we are struggling with today. I feel truly inspired by this album and the opportunity to be a part of its outreach - from organising launch events to liaising with environmental and sustainability charities. For me, this is yet another powerful and innovative way of using music as a global communication tool to do good and an example of pursuing your passion.

Community outreach is essential to me – as well as my projects in the music industry, I am always looking for ways to help others in my job at IBM. I'm currently working on an internal project to aid the practice of music therapy through artificial intelligence. This idea came to me when I noticed that my uncle, who had recently been diagnosed with Alzheimer's, was tapping along to music at one of our family gatherings. He had been struggling with recognition, which our family witnessed, but music seemed to trigger a sense of recognition and pleasure for him – he looked like he was enjoying listening: tapping along to the beat was his way of joining in. Watching my uncle showed me first-hand the role music can play in supporting the needs of patients. So at IBM I am creating an app using our artificial intelligence machine and media capabilities. I want the app to thoroughly meet the needs to the people who are suffering, so I'm working with charities, music therapists, and residential care homes. My ultimate goal is to help people living with dementia relieve symptoms in a fun and stimulating way by successfully connecting my passions for music and technology.

Music is a big part of the community spirit in Gujarati traditions; my love of music began when I was just seven years old and started Indian classical music classes. For my family, it was really important that my sister and I learned about our heritage as a Gujarati family living in England – attending these music classes and Gujarati language lessons at the Bhavan centre was a central way we engaged with our Gujarati culture. As my parents grew up in East Africa, we were part of a community of Gujarati families from East Africa who were now raising their children in London – this mutual connection was very important to all of us, and we could keep in touch with our heritage by sharing traditional Hindu festivities. There was a strong feeling of community, and together we would celebrate Navaratri, the nine-day celebration in October, and Diwali, the festival of lights.

Everything for me is intertwined with my Gujarati heritage; I have been raised by my parents with Gujarati community-driven values. Since birth, I have also had a spiritual connection with the Divine Life Society to which my family are very closely affiliated. My full name is Minal-Radhika Jitendra Mehta – the name 'Radhika' was given to me by my Guru, Swami Chidananda. The Divine Life Society preserves ancient Hindu traditions and cultural practices, and focuses on meditation, spiritual thinking, and spiritual awareness. The headquarters of the Divine Life Society – an ashram set in the foothills of the Himalayas in Rishikesh – is one of my favourite places. When I first visited as a teenager, I was overtaken with a sense of serenity and peace. During my trip, I made an effort to learn about Hinduism and Spirituality by reading books and seeking guidance and mentorship from the Swamijis at the ashram. My spirituality brings me great solace during difficult times. I carry the central values of self-awareness, meditation, and self-reflection with me always – this has helped me in times when I have needed to take a step back and approach hard situations with a clear and focused mind.

My Indian heritage and attending the Bhavan centre meant I was lucky enough to live in two worlds: I had London school life, where I was introduced to English culture and got to understand how people of different backgrounds lived, and I had my Gujarati community, who kept me connected to traditional values. When I was at school, I would go to my friends' houses and see a completely different culture to my own home, and, similarly, my friends got to experience visiting my Indian home and to see my mum cooking Indian food or saying the odd word to me in Gujarati. Both my friends and I were being exposed to new cultures from a young age – I believe this was essential, because integrating with people from all backgrounds is how we grow as a society. When my grandma first moved to England, she would get the odd remark on the street about her outfits because she always wore saris and never switched to Western clothes. “What’s that?” people would say, or “Why are you wearing that?” But she never felt people were hostile, instead, people were asking out of pure curiosity, and she was able to explain to them about her different heritage. In the same way, my grandparents’ neighbours in London helped them to settle into the British way of life and explained to them the different shops or systems so they would be comfortable in their new home.

Sharing my culture and learning about new cultures has given me some of the best times of my life. After growing up in England with Gujarati heritage and parents from East Africa, I completed a degree in French, Spanish and business, during which I lived in both Valencia and Paris. Meeting so many new people and learning about their language and lifestyle was incredible, and I made friends I will keep forever – I really recommend travelling and becoming fully involved with the community where you live. Both my gap year and year abroad taught me how to get along with people from all walks of life.

In my position at IBM, I work with a range of different companies, and my experiences adapting to new cultures when I was younger has made it very easy to communicate with anyone. I joined IBM as a strategy consultant when I finished my degree, and I have since been promoted three times to Managing Consultant for our in-house digital and design agency. I talk to clients from across Europe – I've even been based in Geneva, where I've been able to use my French skills from university to support clients and deliver technology solutions.

Creativity is heightened when you have a diverse team. At IBM, I volunteer for the BAME community and am always looking to build our diversity. The BAME community aims to remove stereotypes, barriers and unconscious bias, which might prevent minority youth from feeling they are capable of following any career path. I'm involved in attracting and engaging BAME talent, leading initiatives such as giving students the opportunity to experience a day in the life of an IBMer, for example through demos of robotics or artificial intelligence. We want to promote STEM (science, technology, engineering, maths or medicine) career paths to BAME students and show them how creative these paths can be. The best workplaces are those where cultural differences are celebrated and people from any background are encouraged to join. More recently, we have been promoting STEM careers to school students from years six to eleven, at around the age they begin thinking about jobs, because this is the time when students could need that extra push or inspiration to realise how many doors there are open to them.

We have reverse mentoring now at IBM, wherein we can educate those above our seniority about what BAME means and how it can help the company, because it's important not to build teams where everyone thinks the same. To help make the workplace feel more welcoming and inclusive, I worked on a project to recruit BAME IBM employees to showcase emerging technologies, such as Blockchain, and then organised a panel of BAME graduates to host a Q&A session with undergraduate students at Kings College, London University. I also organised Diwali celebrations during lunch hour – transforming our canteen with colour, light and mithai (Indian sweets)!

In the last two years, I have been recognised for my efforts to promote inclusivity – I came fifth in the '2018 Fifty Ethnic Minority Future Leader list' presented by Yahoo Finance, and was featured in both the '2018 Empower Fifty Ethnic Minority Future Leader list', presented by the Financial Times, and the '2019 Finalist in Asian Women of Achievement Awards' in Technology & Digital. Winning these awards enabled me to fully develop my interest in supporting BAME youth who want to pursue STEM careers – I have gained recognition as a Role Model and have been invited to speak at universities about my journey into a career in technology. I am now a mentor to BAME undergraduates at London universities and I feel proud to be able to inspire individuals and help them reach the career path they want. I enjoy being able to share my experiences, from missing my university grades to reaching my position at IBM, because this helps students feel comfortable talking with me and relating to me. I find it very rewarding to be able to offer guidance to students. Nobody should ever feel they have to lose sight of their family history, because all heritages are so rich and diverse and different perspectives should be celebrated in the workplace. I volunteer with these inclusivity projects and offer my support as a mentor because I want young people to know it is possible to pursue and achieve your dreams.

CHAPTER 10

Cricket Craze

NAOMI DATTANI

Naomi is a professional cricketer for Sunrisers and a sports coach from Middlesex. She is a captain at Middlesex cricket club in London and has played for Western Storm in the Kia Super league, based in Taunton, in southwest England. At twenty-two Naomi trialled for the England Senior Academy, and her ultimate goal is to play for England.

For Naomi, reaching this goal means working hard and following a dedicated daily routine whilst also balancing her commitments to her family. During her interview, Naomi shared the difficulties she has experienced as a professional British Indian sportswoman and provided incredible insight into ways young women can strive to reach their goals, whatever those may be.

*

"Oh, I don't want to get out by a girl," was one of the many sneers I overheard as a ten-year-old girl playing for my local boys' cricket club. Fortunately, my own teammates were always supportive, but my opponents made it clear they thought I wasn't as good as them because I was a girl. This only made me determined to prove what I was capable of achieving. When my turn came, I bowled six balls and got three wickets, showing these boys, but most importantly, showing myself, that I was a powerful cricket player. In the process, I realised my skills were the best tool to shut those boys up.

Much to our mum's frustration, when my brother and I were growing up we played various sports in our garden – the garden happened to also be my mum's favourite place, so two children racing and rampaging around, breaking pots and damaging plants was irritating for her. Regardless, our beloved garden in Ealing was the first place I played cricket. It was also where my brother told me he saw potential in my cricket skills and encouraged me to join a local team.

I didn't really know that girls played cricket when I first started playing at the local boys' club, but that wasn't important to me. When I proved my strength out on the field to the boys who teased me, I knew girls could play just as well as boys, if not better. I believe their playful mocking only made me a stronger, more determined player. My successes in our games, combined with the support from my brother, teammates, and coach, gave me the confidence I needed to move on to the next stage and trial for Middlesex cricket team when I was eleven – I got in and began playing for Middlesex Girls. It felt great to know I could play well enough to be part of the Middlesex team, and it was exciting to play with other girls who shared my love for cricket. However, as I became more committed to cricket and decided to pursue it as a professional career, I faced even bigger hurdles than those I had dealt with as a young girl.

As a British Indian raised in London with Gujarati values at home, living in two worlds sometimes feels complicated. Family was always marked as a top priority in our Gujarati household, so when I was in school, I balanced school work, cricket, other extracurricular activities, and the family social events which took place, and still take place now, without fail every Saturday. I'd sit down with my school tutor each week and we'd go through my schedule; every day was go, go, go for me from the age of eleven. Cricket was not an essential priority for me in the same way it is now; cricket was one of my favourite hobbies, but my weekly plans also included a range of different activities linking to my Indian heritage. Growing up in England meant we were surrounded by British culture, and for my parents it was important that my brother and I continued to embrace our family's Indian roots. So, as well as always attending our family social events, I played tabla drums for seven years – the tabla is a traditional Indian drum – and went to Gujarati school every Saturday morning. I speak Gujarati fluently and even took my GCSE in Gujarati when I was in school. My life really has always been a balance between

British and Indian culture, and I wouldn't have it any other way.

I think preserving ties to our Indian heritage was especially significant to my mother because she grew up in India, in Gujarat where our family is from. She did not move to England until she was eighteen, although her parents and brother actually moved to England much earlier when she was around eleven. While my mum and her sister stayed in India by themselves and finished their studies, their parents had twin daughters in England. Unlike their older sisters, the twins were raised in the UK and so they were far more adapted to British culture. When my mum and her sister eventually arrived in the UK seven years later, wearing traditional Indian outfits and speaking Gujarati, they must have seemed like aliens to the twins. I can't really imagine how strange it must have been for both pairs of sisters; my mother had no idea how her twin sisters looked as she hadn't seen a photo of them and there they were being raised on another continent. On the other hand, the twins, being ten years younger, were far better adapted to the British language and way of life. My mum and her sister tried to learn English as quickly as they could, but it was difficult for them and their younger sisters would make fun of them. Although now, my mum has adapted well and integrated into the fast pace of British life with the complexities of technology and nuances of the country, she now identifies Britain as her home.

After being raised to follow a particular way of life for the first eighteen years, adapting to a new country and all its nuances was never easy for her.

It's been a rocky road at times for the four sisters and the only brother, but now all of them are very close and even enjoy going on family holidays together. Differences can always be overcome, and we can learn from each other's different strengths: this is how we grow. While my mum and her older sister may have struggled to learn English and to understand British culture in the same way that their siblings do, their upbringing in India focused on more traditional Gujarati roles for women which they have been able to teach the twins. My mother and her sister are talented at cooking, raising a family, and keeping the house in order, and they have passed on their capabilities and life skills to their younger sisters which extends to their children.

Looking after family is so essential to Gujarati beliefs, and my mother and her three sisters all now strongly maintain this value. Gujarati women are taught to prioritise their children and husband and extended family members as well as their in-laws. Their number one focus is their own family and the family they marry into. My mum was raised to be queen of the household; she was brought up to cook so many different types of mouth-wateringly delicious Gujarati dishes, to bring people together in social gatherings, and to make sure everyone else is doing well. My mum never really focuses on herself – her attention is always on others and taking care of everyone else's needs before even thinking about her own. Of course, my mum's approach has really influenced the way I approach things in my own life. I can cook, clean, and take care of my household, and it's really important to me to always make sure everyone around me is feeling comfortable and happy.

Playing professional cricket means that sticking to the typical Gujarati values can sometimes be extremely hard for me. Working as a sportswoman is such a different career path to the typical nine to five job, so it is difficult for my family members to relate to my day-to-day life. When I first started playing cricket as a girl, back in the days when I played for Middlesex Girls, my family was supportive and interested. I think they believed cricket was another of my extracurricular hobbies. Some of my family even came to my games and they'd make a whole day of it – they'd bring a picnic, my mum would make samosas and *chash* (a yoghurt-based drink), and they would sit down and enjoy the game. I think it was a nice day out for them, and it was good for me to have the encouragement.

When I was around sixteen, I made the decision that playing cricket was something I wanted to do professionally. My parents were still coming along to my games to watch and support me, and I felt sure that cricket was an area I could truly achieve success in. As I became more certain about my decision that I wanted cricket to be more than just a hobby, I was selected for the Junior England Pathway. This was the encouragement I needed: it meant I was considered one of the forty best girls at cricket in the country. I was invited to play in a four-day competition, which was a crucial step in my career and a valuable turning point for me; playing in this competition strengthened my decision that I really, really enjoyed playing cricket, and I set my sights on becoming a professional cricket player. Being selected for the pathway also showed me that there were other girls like me who were extremely talented at playing cricket, which motivated me to play as well as I could. Over the four days, as I realised how much I enjoyed the competitive nature, meeting new people, and travelling away from home, I knew this was the career path for me. Choosing this path sometimes means it's very hard to participate in the traditional social events I am expected to attend. Family time is so integral to Gujarati beliefs, and while in my own mind I am always managing the conflict between my Gujarati family values and my rigorous work ethic for cricket, my own family have also found it tough to understand why I can't always join them at family social events.

Playing cricket professionally is a high-pressure job in a variety way to the typical office job, and at times I've found it complicated and tiring to explain these differences to those around me. During every game people who could scout me and move my career forward are watching me so I have to be present at every game and perform at my highest level. It can be hard to explain to people how essential it is that I don't miss out on any games or any training. My mum is supportive, but when I feel sick or injured, she will tell me to take a day off and rest – this isn't possible when playing a professional sport. I need to train every day and stay on top of my game; if I lose a day due to sickness or a sore leg or even attending a social event, this sets me back because other players will not have taken that day off. I face weekly challenges from the clashes between dedicating myself to cricket and trying to meet my Gujarati family expectations, but I know that to achieve my goals I must put my sport first. I am willing to make sacrifices on a week by week basis, and as time passes and I achieve more success my family are growing more accepting of my choices.

I am expected to be the queen of the household, but I also want to be the most powerful player out on the pitch. Playing cricket and being a sports coach does not really fit in with the typical ideas of what is expected from a young woman in an Indian family. Stereotypically, careers include being a lawyer, a doctor, and working in business or technology, so being a sportswoman differs greatly from what's expected of me. I think being a woman makes it especially difficult for my sports career to be taken seriously, and it has taken me a long time to prove to people that this is a viable career. I've learned to be strong and just accept that it may take some people longer than others understand my different path, but not to let this impact my own acceptance of myself and my own belief in my capabilities.

The most important piece of advice I could give to any young girl who wants to be successful at what they are doing is to invest in themselves. I made the decision that cricket was what I wanted to do, and ever since I have been making choices which will help me reach my goals as a cricket player. I decided to go to the University of Loughborough to study Sports and Exercise Science, because I wanted to be in a place where I could play and improve my cricket skills. Invest in yourself. Put yourself first, and work out everything else later. This is definitely easier said than done, and for me, putting myself first feels like a selfish thing to do, but one of the most crucial lessons I've learnt is that it is not selfish to strive for my goals. If you really want something, you need to make those crucial choices and personal investments. Regardless of what people think now, once they see your success they will no longer be critical, they'll be congratulating you – so never let anyone's opinion dictate your decisions. Remind yourself you are doing what is best for you, and therefore it is not selfish it is just what you need to do to achieve your goals. Every decision I've made is in line with my goals – I've worked hard to invest in university and find sponsors so that I can be supplied with the cricket equipment I need. To be successful at anything, you need to be organised and focused.

Once I graduated from university, I faced another major turning point in my career. Coaches kept asking me what I was going to do with the potential I had now that I was finished with my studies. All I could think was, 'the last thing I want to say to myself ten years from now is that I regret not trying.' I made the decision to push myself forward, and I went to Australia for six months to play cricket. In Australia my sole focus was cricket; I trained every single day and played for a club. Playing with so many different people and experiencing several challenges allowed me to have the best season I have ever had. Making this choice to take a risk and concentrate on improving my skills showed me I was capable of achieving what is now my ultimate goal: playing for England. When I returned from Australia, I was selected to play multiple games for the England senior academy. My experience was peculiar as I felt like and imposter and I often asked myself: "What am I doing here?!" I had not comprehended how much I had improved and that took time to process. Self-investment allowed me to move a step closer to my final goal, and I will continue to invest in my talent until I reach it.

When playing professional sport, things can change so quickly. You always have to be ready and perform when the opportunities arise; you are never far away from being spotted or selected and having your entire career moved forward. I've found that working hard and creating routines with small daily things to improve on is what leads to success. I call these small goals the 'one percenters', and I believe that if you complete your one percenters every day you will get closer and closer to your ultimate goal. The one percenter can be really small, it could be as simple as drinking three litres of water a day, but one percenters are essential because they are the things which help you stay healthy, stick to a regular pattern, and feel calmer and more confident that you are doing what is right for you. It is a type of meditation; installing such routines and habits in your life will be incredibly helpful for anything you want to achieve.

Each day, one of my one percenters is writing in my journal – it is my vision board and it is how I remind myself of what I am working towards. I would advise anyone who is striving towards a goal to keep a journal wherein they place their goal at the forefront. I landed with a six-week contract for Western Storm, where I played professionally in the Kia Super League. I would write down daily reminders to myself that this was one of my goals. Writing down your goals will help you believe in what you can do. Now, I write down every day that I will play for England; this is my target, and with every single one percenter that I maintain in my life I will increase my chances of reaching it. Sometimes, I may even need to write reminders to myself to do something fun to enjoy myself; writing in my journal allows me to express that I deserve to relax and take the pressure off myself from time to time. I enjoy cricket – there are three distinct reasons why I play: firstly I love the outdoors, secondly my undeniable love for competing, and finally my passion for playing with a wide range of different people. I have enjoyed the opportunity to play across the world in countries like South Africa, Dubai, India and Australia and that's been an exhilarating experience for me. Whenever I remind myself of why I enjoy cricket, I find my motivation and it propels me towards achieving my goals - it's my purpose.

As well as offering me with an exciting career, playing cricket has allowed me to provide my services as an athletic volunteer and to help others come together through sport. I discovered how helpful sports can be for working in a community whilst volunteering on a trip to South Africa run by Balls for Poverty in 2014, a charity which is run by a football coach who works for the FA. It was the tenth year that Balls for Poverty had been delivering football, rugby, and general sports teamwork sessions to different towns in South Africa, Kenya, and Uganda. We brought together children who were living rough lives and tried to help them enjoy some exercise and practice teamwork. Some places we visited were very dangerous and filled with gang violence, knife crime, and drugs, but organising these sporting events allowed the children to have some calm moments.

One town we visited had a vast spread of green land which was filled with different gang members and had a tense, hostile atmosphere. Fights broke out regularly. Fortunately, our charity leader was familiar with the leaders of the three main gangs from his previous trips, and they were all willing to come together and play a football match against each other when we set up our equipment. We organised a football match, and as soon as we did so, a diverse group of people began joining in and started to enjoy kicking the ball around with one another. Players from different gangs were shaking hands and putting away their guns; feeling the environment shift away from hostility was a really touching moment, and unlike anything I had experienced before.

Watching our sporting activities help others made me realise the potential I have to help others with my time and skills. Participating in such an experience has irreversibly changed my life for the better. I encourage everyone to participate in charity work. I know for certain that when I am finished with my sporting career I will strive to do more volunteering. For now I am honoured to be awarded a professional contract with the Sunrisers and being in a unique position out of the forty cricketers in the UK. I am exclusively focusing on my fulltime job, training to maximise my athletic performance through my mental and physical resilience. I know how lucky I am and have been to be born in a country where I have access to everything I need and which allows me to work on achieving my goals.

CHAPTER 11

Feel Good with Lavina

LAVINA MEHTA MBE

Lavina Mehta MBE is a 42-year-old British Asian award-winning personal trainer and mum of three. Lavina has been awarded an MBE for services to health and fitness during the Covid-19 pandemic. Her mission is to help people feel good physically, mentally and emotionally.

Lavina's brand, 'Feel Good with Lavina', follows on from her mother's last book which she helped publish: 'Feel Good with Food', a vegetarian cookbook which focuses on eating healthily combined with the science behind food. During our interview, Lavina talked about her own wellness journey, and how important exercise and healthy eating are for reducing the risk of chronic diseases. We discussed the challenges she faced when she was working as a businesswoman in Canary Wharf and unexpectedly fell in love and quickly became a wife and mother. Having left her corporate career as a global project manager, after having her son who is now a teenager, Lavina requalified over three years ago and has been training women one-to-one, in groups, in her virtual online community and globally via her Online Training App. She passionately promotes the health benefits of exercise on TV and radio, including her ingenious concept of 'Exercise Snacking'.

During lockdown she provided free twice-daily virtual workouts with her family for people of all ages and continues to provide specially designed virtual chair workouts to help thousands of elderly and vulnerable people to stay fit, physically and mentally, from home. Her slogan is to 'Exercise for Sanity not Vanity'. Lavina also works with businesses to promote workplace wellness and encourages working out from home during the unprecedented pandemic era.

She has found her purpose in life as a leader in fitness especially with the Asian community, which brings her enormous joy and helps a huge number of people on their wellness journey.

*

Our true passions aren't always found immediately. I became a personal trainer when I was already a mother to three boys and had previously had a career in management. I think mothers, especially, can feel a little lost after having children, but once they start to get a bit older and we have more time to ourselves, new interests can develop, changing our lives. I have been helping people become fitter and live a healthier, happier lifestyle - I have completely switched gears from my senior management role and am truly passionate about the incredible mental and physical benefits of exercising. Having multiple career paths throughout life can be a really positive thing - as we change and grow, it seems inevitable that our passions will too.

Going to the gym was something I started to do as a hobby every day after dropping my sons off at school. At first, it was quite a social thing - I would go to a class and then have a coffee and chat, but I grew more and more interested in exercising, and found my own personal trainer. He demonstrated the benefits of weight-training, and so I moved on from the classes to start focusing on weights and increasing my strength, which came hand-in-hand with more discipline and focus on healthy eating. I started taking a home study course in fitness instructing, a level two qualification, because I loved what it was doing for my body and mind and I wanted to learn more for my own training. After finishing university, I thought I would never sit another exam in my life, let alone want to spend my evenings studying after the children were asleep, but I loved the fitness course. I completed it in my own time because I felt so passionate.

It felt natural after completing my level two to start my level three qualification, which allowed me to become a certified personal trainer. I kept it mostly to myself that I was doing this training, because I didn't want any pressure, I just wanted to study what I loved. Before I even qualified, people started messaging me with their interest in having training sessions. We have a home gym in our basement, so I decided to start using this to help women train on their wellness journey. I started by giving private one-to-one sessions at home, which really appealed to women who didn't want to go to the gym for a number of different reasons, including perhaps feeling intimidated by other people watching them.

As a coach, I am not just interested in my clients' fitness, I help them improve their health as a whole. This means eating and sleeping well, exercising, and having positive, sustainable lifestyle habits. I have loved helping women with all of the challenges we face, from hormonal changes, to post childbirth, to menopause; there is so much we can go through in life, and exercise is always beneficial. Some women may be slender for their whole lives, but have never been serious about exercise - I think we need to be more aware of that, whatever our natural body size, we need to stay fit, because this is can really help reduce risks of all the chronic diseases which are growing more prevalent in society. My training is not about hardcore weight loss, it's about feeling good and improving mental health. I've had so many women say to me that starting exercise has changed their mood, helped them sleep better, made them more flexible and stronger, be a better person - these aren't all things we can see, it's not about aesthetics, it's about a complete mental and lifestyle shift and introducing more positivity into our everyday lives.

I left my management career behind when I had my youngest son and this background has been incredibly useful in building my own business as a personal trainer, influencing a huge number of people through virtual training. We are always building upon different skills we already possess, even if we don't realise. My management training means I'm very thorough and organised, and I pride myself in dedicating time to writing every client a personal plan and creating structured programmes to really make a difference. As I progressed, I was alarmed by the statistics which indicated that Asians are less physically active, with a higher risk of diabetes and heart disease, in comparison to the white population. I have been promoting the health benefits of exercise to treat, prevent and reduce risks of these rising chronic diseases on national news channels, radio and my social media platforms. Just before lockdown I launched a national campaign to "Get UK Asians Fit".

Starting to exercise can feel really daunting if you've never done it before, and maybe you don't know where to start or think it's going to take up lots of time which you don't have. To help with this, I came up with the idea of exercise snacking - short bouts or 'bites' of exercise throughout your day to treat your body and mind. My *exercise snacks*, include 'Feel Good Walk Snacks' and 'Stair Snacks' which are perfect home solutions for keeping the body moving. My family workouts, for all ages, cover my fitness prescription of mobility, cardio, strength training and stretch. During lockdown I also created a 'Feel Good in 5/10 minutes' workout series. My slogan through the Covid-19 pandemic was to 'Exercise for Sanity not Vanity' and I also provided a free *Feel Good 21 Day Workout Plan*. I want to make exercise fun, accessible and easy for all ages and all levels!

I have had the pleasure of leading thousands of elderly people during the pandemic with keeping fit and combating loneliness by becoming part of my feel good community. Studies show how exercise can help prevent the effects of so many chronic illnesses like Alzheimer's, Type 2 diabetes, osteoporosis, heart disease and types of cancers, and I always strive to make it easy for people to include exercise into their everyday lives. My free virtual home workouts for seniors, in English and Gujarati, with my 73-year-old mother in law, have really helped to inspire thousands of elderly community members globally. I have committed to give back to the disproportionately affected Asian communities by providing these specially designed virtual chair workouts to help the vulnerable stay fit, physically and mentally. They have embraced technology and join in with me via Zoom, YouTube and my social media platforms, with many using my saved YouTube workouts as part of their daily routine, from home without any fancy equipment. Even my own mother now fits in her snack walks whenever she can each day to keep fit, using whatever ten minutes or more that she has here or there.

My mother herself is a huge inspiration to me, and we have embraced our health and wellness journeys with food and exercise together. My mother is also a woman who changed careers and found her passion after dedicating so much time to raising her children. Both of my parents have Gujarati heritage and were raised in Mombasa in Kenya. My mother moved to London from Mombasa to live with her sister when she was only sixteen, to study her A-Levels and was the first Asian woman to graduate with a degree in biological sciences from the University of East Anglia in 1969. Like many that moved here in the 1960s, my parents invested in their education, worked hard and started from scratch. My mum met my dad on a trip back to Mombasa when he sold her a plane ticket home, as he was chartering flights from England back to Mombasa at the time. His natural talent as an entrepreneur helped him from an early age to support his studies. After they got married, my mother began helping my dad in his travel business until she had children when she stayed at home with me and my brother. They prioritised and sacrificed so much for our schooling and education. However, biological sciences was never truly left behind, because, as my brother and I got older and she had more time to herself, a great passion of my mother's became clear: cooking, and the science behind food. She became a cookery teacher and started writing for the BBC Good Food magazine, as well as doing consultancy for the late Linda McCartney and having her own vegetarian cookbook published. When I was on maternity leave and decided not to go back to work, my mother and I decided to put another book together. This time she wanted to research about super foods and antioxidants and why different foods really are good for your health - here, her scientific training combined with her amazing cooking abilities meant she could research how to eat healthily and simply explain how diseases and cancers could be prevented and reduced by eating a good diet.

My brand, 'Feel Good with Lavina', stems from with my mother's book, 'Feel Good with Food', which I helped her with as a sous-chef, photographer and typist. While I was still breast-feeding my new-born son at my parents' house, she was cooking for everyone and we were writing the recipes to turn them into a book. I love being creative, so I helped her with the styling, designs and photos of the food and, we self-published the book. Watching her cook and listening to all of the research she had done gave me so much insight into nutrition and understanding why food is so important - this has been incredibly beneficial for my own wellness journey and helping my clients, because fitness and healthy eating go hand in hand. The famous quotation of Hippocrates the father of modern medicine, inspired her to write this book: "Let your food be your medicine, let your medicine be your food." Now one of my slogans is: "Use exercise as medicine!"

Our family's Jain principles tie in perfectly with living a healthy and enriching life; Jain principles mean living without violence and being kind to others. Physical and mental wellness derive from many things, but with a negative or hostile attitude and a closed heart, it will be much harder to achieve happiness. In addition to exercise and healthy eating, practicing Jain principles of kindness and generosity helps me to feel good. Our family is vegetarian, and my mother's cooking focuses on eating a nutritious colourful vegetarian diet filled with health benefits.

Jain monks can be incredibly strict - while all Jains are vegetarian, some monks will wear masks so they don't breathe in any organisms, they will boil their water, and they don't eat root vegetables. In strict Jainism, anything which has a root form of life is valued and not allowed to be eaten. These monks fast for long periods of time, and believe that everything is based on karma and, eventually, they will be liberated and reincarnated to live in *Moksha*, meaning liberation from the cycle of birth, death, and rebirth altogether. The British playwright George Bernard Shaw said: "I adore so greatly the principles of the Jain religion that I would like to be reborn in a Jain community."

After my mother lost her dad when she was only sixteen, my grandmother pledged to live a solitary life and turned to religion. My grandmother tried to commit to a lot of the strict Jain rituals, praying for hours every day and eating only during daylight hours.

It was harder to fully live a Jain lifestyle outside of India, but she was very dedicated, and she fasted often, and completed *Ayambil* - fasting for the longest time anyone had in our community in Mombasa. I would say I am a modern Jain; I apply what I can in my life in England, but we have adapted the principles here, and focus strongly on treating people how we want to be treated. I would like my children to be raised with these basic principles of non-violence, and I encourage them to pray, too, as I do every night, and when we go to our centre in Potters Bar, they participate in religious ceremonies with our family. My mother-in-law also encourages and inspires us with her devotion to Jain religion and reminds me a lot of my late grandmother. The seniors' workout sessions she agreed to do with me for the elderly during the pandemic align with Jain principles and are a form of seva (selfless service), which helped persuade and motivate her to join me. She would never have had the confidence or imagined being on Zoom, YouTube or featured on national radio and TV, but the thousands of messages we have received about how these workouts have helped individuals combat loneliness, exercise and stay healthy from home have made us more determined to continue and give back.

Any trip to India by my mum or close family would involve embarking on a pilgrimage up into the mountains to one of Jain's oldest temples in Palitana in Gujarat. It's an incredible journey; in the morning, you wake up and have to climb thousands of steps. At this extraordinary height up in the mountains, it feels like being in heaven. I have always wondered how they managed to build it so high up in the mountains. It's a very meaningful place for our family, and my husband and I have taken our children there.

When I was growing up, even though we lived in England, our parents were great at keeping us close to our Gujarati heritage. Saturday and Sunday mornings were spent going to Gujarati school, and I actually completed my Gujarati GCSE, which was amazing because it meant I could communicate in Gujarati really well and I would exchange letters with my grandmother. I also did Kathak, a classical Indian dance and learned to play the harmonium - I absolutely loved performing on stage. When I was eleven, I travelled to India alone and spent the summer with my aunt and uncle. It seems incredible now that I travelled all that distance by myself when I was so young, but it was the best experience I could have gained because I became completely immersed in the Gujarati culture. I spent two of my summers as a young girl in India in my aunt's family home and loved having private art lessons at home with a local teacher. That is where my love for painting began. Throughout my childhood, my mum would take me to art galleries and exhibitions every school holiday and this helped me excel in A Level Art. I wanted to pursue it as a career and although I went on to complete a degree in management, my mum always encouraged me to keep up this life skill and when the children were all at school I went back to painting as a hobby, to create many pieces for my home and friends and family. Like exercise I find it very therapeutic.

During those summers travelling alone, I also learnt a very long, complicated Indian prayer, which I have been asked to recite at large community events over the last few years. It's one of our longest prayers, and it's often said by elderly people, so members of my community were quite shocked that a young girl like me knew how to say it. I sing it like a song, almost like a modern song instead of spoken like a typical prayer, and it has so much meaning to the Jain community. When my grandmother passed away from Alzheimer's disease, I had not sung the prayer in years, but last minute at her funeral I decided that I wanted to recite the prayer. I stood up, closed my eyes, and somehow recited all twenty-four verses, I'm sure my grandmother guided me through it.

My parents were one of only two Indian families on their street when they bought their house in Golders Green in London. The neighbourhood is more culturally diverse now, but it used to be a very orthodox Jewish neighbourhood as I grew up. I feel, and my Jewish friends also feel, that I can blend very easily with the Jewish community; culturally, Gujarati and Jewish values have a lot in common, as we are both very family oriented, and I never really felt any racism from any Jewish people in our area. My dad's business partner also moved into the house next door to us, so we had close family friends and we would visit every day and spend time with each other. It was a welcoming home where lots of relatives were always popping in and out, and I feel very lucky that we didn't experience any discrimination.

While there are many incredible aspects to Indian communities, sometimes taboo topics and specific expectations for women can be really difficult. I hope that by sharing my story I can show other women that they are not alone. When I met my husband, we fell head over heels in love very quickly, and even though I was twenty-four, at a great place in my career, I decided to get married. With my job, I was commuting into Canary Wharf every day and working in a senior global role that was very time-consuming. I decided to fight for part-time work, which, for someone in a senior position, was relatively unheard of at the time, but my boss was very supportive and managed to get me a job share. I worked extremely hard Wednesdays to Fridays and tried to find some work life balance to have enough time to help with my new joint family life.

When I became pregnant with our third son, I decided not to go back to work after I went on maternity leave. It was a challenging moment leaving a job I loved, but I wanted to be there at home for all three of my children and put all my energy into being a mother. Being a mother has been the most rewarding experience and I know from my own upbringing how important it was to have my mother investing all her time into our education, encouraging activities, hobbies and culture and giving us an all-round loving upbringing. Now, of course, my sons are older, and I totally switched careers to work in personal training once they were all settled in their respective schools. I can't wait to see what the future holds with my work. I think my business is quite unique because I'm not selling anything and, blessed with my husband providing us with security, I am not financially driven. I am very lucky that I have such a supportive husband, children and family that encourage and champion me to pursue my dreams with work, as they can see it's my passion and purpose.

My motivation and mission is simple: to help as many people as possible to feel good physically and mentally. So many people could benefit from learning about how to reduce their risks of chronic diseases by exercising, and I hope the honour of receiving an MBE will help me reach more people and continue promoting these benefits on an even larger scale. My aim to help people get healthy and stay fit, feels quite personal since I lost my father-in-law, an amazing man, without whom I would not have been able to raise my children, as he was my rock and he had an incredible aura. He believed in helping those less fortunate and giving back and did so much charity work including organising incredible global 'Cycling for Charity' events. He died from a sudden brain tumour which hit him very severely and he lost his mobility and his speech within just six months. Having seen this first-hand as we lived next door and did everything for him, has fuelled my passion further. Unfortunately, I think a lot of people in my generation are seeing their parents or relatives suffer from such illnesses, so I am hoping I can try and especially educate and influence the Asian community even more.

Even as a female, a wife or a mother in the Asian community, it is often seen as selfish to exercise and invest in your health. There is so much expectation around self-sacrifice for the good of the family and to care for those around us. I think things are changing with an increasing awareness of health, and that it's important for women to focus on their own wellbeing and selfcare, which will also benefit everyone around them.

There are still huge taboos around discussing health issues; we need to be more open about our personal experiences, to help spread awareness of health problems. I recently went on Sky News to talk about a smear test I had when I was twenty-six which showed that I had abnormal cells. I was diagnosed with mild dyskaryosis, but it was at a very early stage, it was pre-cervical cancer, and I had to have laser treatment to remove them. This was a scary experience for me. A lot of people don't attend their smear tests - of course, it's not something that's very comfortable to go through - but it is incredibly important to catch things early, and so it's important to be open and talk about issues we have. Exercise plays a huge part in reducing risks of cancer, and I think this personal health scare really shaped and initiated my wellness journey, as I hadn't put much effort into exercise and eating healthily before.

My main message is that exercise doesn't have to be difficult or cost anything. Find something you enjoy and I guarantee it will make you feel good. Try snacking on exercise through the day, it's the healthiest form of snacking around! That may be as easy as doing a 10-minute walk snack after each meal or doing a stair snack by climbing three flights of stairs, three times a day! I encourage everyone to start off small and gradually build up to hitting the government guidelines for optimum health by doing two or three strength training workouts a week, as well as 150 minutes of moderate intensity or 75 minutes of vigorous intensity aerobic activity per week. We need to keep our muscles strong by staying physically active which will also keep our immune system strong. Health should be our main priority especially after a global pandemic like Covid-19 and not just our physical health but mental health. As I say: 'Lets exercise for sanity not vanity.' Looking after ourselves through movement and eating nutritious, fresh, colourful food packed with antioxidants has endless benefits for our body and mind. While it can be really difficult to make that first step and start, exercise will reward you in ways you may never have imagined.

Fill your life with joy and love, fulfil your dreams, it makes life worth living and remembering.

CHAPTER 12

Pure Soul

HEENA SHAH

Heena is a leader in her field of event design and management in London. Her entrepreneurial skills are applied to lead an outstanding team which boasts over 18 years' experience in designing and producing spectacular events. She's the founder of Event Gurus and together with her husband Nilesh, they collaborate and deliver bespoke designs and much more for corporate and private clients, from global conferences at Latimer House, award Ceremonies at Grosvenor House to weddings at Blenheim Palace.

When I met Heena to hear her story, I had little idea what she was going to reveal. Her story uncovers the plight of immigrants from Gujarat to the enormous tragedy of losing her father and child. I was left inspired by her remarkable spirit and resilience in dealing with her loss and determination in realising her vision for her family and business.

*

The grief of losing my baby at thirty-eight weeks gripped me for so long, I felt that eventually I had to let her go. Her soul was pure and maybe she's needed elsewhere. I am Heena and a mother of three children.

In 2011, my life changed in moments, from expecting my second child to returning home, empty arms. It turned my world upside down and left me devastated. The pain I felt when I lost my father back in 1997 was hugely intense and it clouded me yet again when I lost my baby.

My father was born in Kenya and he married my mother, who was from Uganda. After their marriage, they stayed in Mombasa for a few months after I was born. I was a mere six months old when we boarded a ship to take us to India. We stayed in Gujarat for about a year, which is where my dad became attached to his ancestral land.

It was a family decision eventually to leave India, to travel to a third continent and settle in the UK for a better life, on the south coast of England in Brighton. My mother's brothers had already established a base there; it was 1976. A tough time for immigrants, especially if you were Indian and in the minority. Then to acclimatise to the weather, food and to learn the language was a huge challenge in itself.

The isolation felt by my grandmother with a loss of socialising within her community in Mombasa and in Gujarat was heart-breaking for her. My father took a decisive step to relocate so that he could be closer to his work in Luton and to provide his mother with the Asian community that she craved.

Whilst growing up in Luton, it was in my secondary school that I first started experiencing racism. Such incidents are never that easy to erase from your mind. I remember when my parents had worked exceptionally hard and bought me a beautiful jacket that I just loved. It was lunchtime, when this girl who was with her group of friends approached me calling me a 'paki' and taunting me for having black hair and brown skin. The girls were older than me, and I dared not correct or challenge them. I was disgusted when one of the girls took her cigarette and stubbed it out on my new jacket, burning a hole into the fabric. I wasn't upset that there was now a hole in it, but the fact that my parents had worked so hard to buy this jacket, it was a precious sentiment for me. I was so upset that I didn't go home for lunch that day and went back to school on an empty stomach. I managed to stitch the hole together and somehow repair the damage so that it would go unnoticed. People think they can get away with this kind of behaviour, because they believe it's their country, and only their country. What did I do wrong, where was my identity?

Our family had their economic struggles just like many immigrants at that time. My dear mother worked in a factory making television components and it was an intensive strain on her eyes. My father worked long hours to provide for the family and both my parents stood united in ensuring that my brother and I were instilled with the best cultural values and education. In our three-bedroom house, sharing a room with my grandmother meant we had a lot of fun - we used to stay up late, and she would tell me stories about the Ramayana and the Bhagavad Gita, whilst joyfully snacking on 'chevda' (Bombay mix), and there'd to be so much noise coming from our room that my father would tell me off about not going to sleep on time. This beautiful precious bond is what I hope my children will continue to have with their grandparents, and one that can be replicated with my future grandchildren. Living with my grandmother as I grew up was amazing for a multitude of reasons, including the influence she had on the type of food we ate: she cooked fresh, healthy meals for us all the time and passed down Gujarati recipes. She enriched our lives by encouraging us to be part of so many wonderful Hindu traditions such as celebrating Diwali together. I can proudly pass these great values to my children and beyond.

My children call their grandmother at 7.30am every morning on their way to school, every day religiously, and they speak to her in Gujarati. When someone elderly comes to the house, they always treat them with respect - and know how to greet, converse and serve them well.

It's very important to me that my children learn positive cultural and social values. Both my children have attended faith-based primary schools where worship at the temple is within their timetable. My daughter now attends secondary school in Northwood where the culture is diverse. With the solid foundation she has attained through her education and family life, any negative influences interrupting her life are eradicated quickly because she has a clear moral compass and can distinguish clearly between right and wrong.

There is a time and place for everything. I strongly believe that we should give one hundred percent to everything that we do. When my children were younger, I gave up my city job and I dedicated my time to them because they needed me - as they grew older, I had more time on my hands and I was able to put my time and energy into other initiatives. One of the most important being my Rickshaw Run Charity fundraiser. As my children's independence grows my role as a mother continues to evolve. There is often so much pressure to balance different aspects of life and to deliver everything perfectly. But it's ok to let something drop, it's fine not to attend all the parties, it's fine not to be seen on social media, I have always done what suits my environment.

I have been an advocate of charity work for a long time, as a practicing Hindu the concept of Sewa has been engrained in our upbringing and daily life. It's only now my capacity has increased that I can give more back to society. Our rickshaw run was a twelve-day, 2500km journey across India in an auto-rickshaw, raising money for the charity Cochlea which supports deaf children in India. At the time Cochlea was building a medical centre which can prescribe deaf children with implants that enable them to hear. My daughter said her first word at nine months, and I met a mother in India on our journey whose own daughter had not said her first word until she was six years old! As time goes on, if a child has a hearing impairment, this can often cause problems for their speech too, so another function of the medical centre is to provide speech therapy for deaf children who need this.

I recall a memorable conversation with my seven-year-old son while I was checking in at the airport. He said to me: "So mummy, is it important to help your son or other children?" I kneeled down so that I was eye level with him and explained: "It's important to help everyone. I help you daily, and they need help too. I am not going to stay with them for seven years." He might not always understand why I am giving time to other children, but I know that I give enough time to my own children, and I feel I have the ability to increase my capacity for who I am caring for, and the ability to give more to charities as well as my own family. Ninety of us from all over the world took part on the rickshaw run for Cochlea where Sewa UK helped raise over £250,000, and that money will be used for building, teaching, training, providing equipment and accommodation for these children. My son and daughter came out to meet me at the finish line in India: they were so happy and proud to see me. My daughter was very inspired by the journey I had made, and I hope that she can start her own sewa contribution for communities.

Before we had any children, my husband Nilesh and I set up our own business. As the eldest granddaughter in my house, I always tell my younger relatives to study hard, get a job, but then, whilst doing a job, start another business. It will be really hard, it will be a lot of work, but it will be worth it because once you have your children, your business is already established, you will be able to stop working for someone else and work for yourself. This gives you the quality time and flexibility to be with your child when they need you.

Our business started one late afternoon in Gujarat, shortly after Nilesh and I had got married. It was 2002, after the 9/11 terrorist attacks, so the financial and IT sector which we worked in were plummeting, and there were riots in Gujarat, meaning there were imposed curfews happening around the state. As we walked to the train station one late afternoon, we came across this wedding shop in an alleyway and we thought: "Should we start doing wedding invitations as a side business?" It was a spur of the moment idea, and we had a train to catch so we quickly rushed inside and asked the owner if he could send some samples to see if the invites would appeal to people in England. We gave him our address and started our journey back to England.

Within a week of returning to the UK, we received a stack of sample invitation cards. I was so excited. That year, our first year as a business, we had fifty different weddings to produce bespoke invitation cards for. Initially, it was all from friends and family as word spread that we were doing invites as our side business, and at the weekends we would print the invites at home. We would receive samples from India and typeset it ourselves. We were able to expand our business and provide 'mandaps' (a covered structure with pillars serving as an alter for Hindu weddings) for hire as well as other wedding furniture.

My work ethics are modelled on my mother and father, who put so much effort into making our lives better in England. To live and support the extended family and to be socially active in the community.

When I was twenty-one, my dad decided to take six weeks off and travel to India with me and my brother. He was so excited to show us around his motherland, meet the extended family and enjoy the culture. No one knew that this was going to be his last journey and life changing for me. My father and his cousins had invested their hard-earned money in properties in Gujarat, and he was looking forward to taking possession of the keys. My nani (my mum's mum) travelled with us and we left her with her relatives in Mumbai. My dad was her favourite, and their relationship as mother-in-law and son-in-law was very unique. We dropped the excess luggage, connected with our friends from London who were going to join us on the trip. We all headed to Mount Abu in Rajasthan, a rocky, elevated hill area surrounded by rich, deep green forest with a bright turquoise lake below. The climate was cool and on day three after arriving we were on our way down the hill after a morning of hiking. Despite the chill, I noticed that my father was sweating. “Why are you sweating?” we asked, and when we looked at him closely, we could see his eyes had rolled back, and only the whites of his eyes could be seen. That was quite frightening as we hadn’t seen that happen before. He managed to inform us that he wasn’t feeling well, and so he laid down in the car. We started to drive, but suddenly my dad wanted to get out of the car - when he did, he collapsed. As we picked my dad up, he started to say he needed to use the toilet, but we were in the middle of nowhere so we had to knock on the door of a random house and ask if our dad could use the toilet. They were nice enough and let him in, he went to the toilet, walked around the courtyard, and then said: “Let’s go.” We carried on driving, but his eyes rolled again, and by now we had arrived in Udaipur and drove straight to the hospital. The second we arrived at the hospital, the staff told us: “No, you can’t bring him in, he needs to go to a doctor first.” We quickly helped our dad get back in the car again and sped off to visit a doctor. These were some of the bizarre complexities of the Indian medical system that we experienced back then.

"He's had a heart attack." The doctor said, as soon as he took a look at my dad. "You have got to take him to hospital." We helped him out of the doctors' surgery and back into the car where he asked: "What's happened?" "Nothing," I said, "they just need to check you out," and we started driving back to the hospital, got him a wheelchair, but it was broken, so we had to put him over our shoulders and walk as quickly as we could over to the intensive care unit. We showed them the letter from the doctor and they let him into a hospital room, where the doctor laid him down and showed us a big list. "What's this?" I asked. "This is all the medication that you need," the doctor replied. It was a list of cotton wool, an oxygen tank, needles, everything. "Okay," I said, "but can you start the treatment first while we pay?" He looked at me and told me: "No. We will need all of this, and you need to register him first." So I stayed with my dad while my brother went to register him. Our family friend who had travelled with us ran to the pharmacy next door and bought all the stuff to start the treatment. By the time we had got everything ready, my dad had another heart attack and passed away.

My father's last words were just "Heena, Heena, Heena," as if he didn't want to go, but he just went. On the first of December at 1pm I lost my father forever. I just remember thinking: "How is this even possible?" We rang my mum's younger brother in Brighton and told him what had happened, and instantly he said: "Okay, we are going to Luton." "Don't say anything to mum just yet," we told him. In the meantime, we contacted our insurance company for advice, and they instructed us to let the hospital follow the normal procotol and take him to the mortuary and that they would take over the procedure from there. They told us to take care of ourselves and head home and they would bring our dad home within between eight and twenty-one days. It was at this point that we discovered that there wasn't a cold mortuary in the hospital, because in India they usually do a cremation on the same day. With no ice facility and very high risk of the body decomposing we knew we had to do something. We had to get dad back home. Ringing the insurance company again, they told us that it would take eight days at the earliest until they could transport him, and that if we touched the body, it would no longer be their liability. We packed our dad's body with ice and hired a private charter plane to take us to Mumbai, so that we could get on an international flight back home with British Airways. The flight didn't leave until the next day, so that night, my brother and I had to take shifts standing outside the mortuary to keep an eye on our dad's body to make sure nobody took body parts or organs from him. These are valuable assets in India. We took turns standing there all night. In the morning, we realised that coffins aren't standard in India. So we had to measure up dad's body, buy wood, nails, and find a carpenter to build a coffin. When the charter plane to Mumbai arrived, on a random airstrip in the middle of a field, we patiently stood for the cargo door to open but, there was no cargo door, the cargo door was the passenger door, so when we tried to get the coffin in, it wouldn't fit. We had no other choice but to lay a sheet down next to us on the plane, and carefully take our dad out of the coffin and lay him at our feet to get him to Mumbai. We had to make two calls before departing one was to the funeral directors requesting another coffin and the other call was to my nani's relatives to explain the situation and get her to the airport without telling her what had happened. As soon as we landed my nani asked where my father was. I said: "He is coming, he is with us."

We had one more step to overcome before we could get back to the UK: getting clearance from the local funeral director - Mr Pinto. "It's all cleared," he told us, "but you have to give me $1,200 in cash before I can stamp the final clearance." It was two o'clock in the morning by this point. We told him we didn't have dollars, but he just said: "Well, go and get it converted." British Airways had waited patiently for us while we raced to get the $1,200 in cash and pay the sum demanded. All the way home on that flight, my nani cried. She was completely devasted and shocked.

I vividly remember that journey back to Luton after we got off the plane and the British funeral company took over from us. We were near junction 9 on the M1, going down a hill, and all we could see was green countryside for miles. I felt so small, thinking: "What are you doing in this world?" and wondering how I was going to face my mum. In India, if you cry you automatically become weak, and in this situation, we didn't have time to become weak. For ten years, I couldn't talk about what happened to my dad because it was so upsetting.

The pain parents feel when they outlive their child is hard to bear. Living in a modern country with health facilities at one's disposal, I actually felt safe until I suffered the heartbreaking loss of my second baby. The house was ready, the room was ready, the feeding station was ready, and my daughter Simi was only four years old at the time and she helped me throughout the pregnancy and the excitement of preparing everything.

She thought she was going to have a sister coming home.

I was thirty-eight weeks pregnant when I woke up, spotting of blood, even though I wasn't in any pain, I thought I must be in labour. I woke my husband and told him we had to go to the hospital. As we were driving, I could feel the baby moving the whole way there. We arrived at the maternity ward and I was first seen by a nurse in triage. The nurse attached a monitor then went away and came back with another nurse. She fiddled with the machine, went away and came back with another machine. They still could not find what they were looking for. Then another doctor and nurse came along to the bedside. The doctor fiddled with the second machine and told us they could not find the heartbeat. I told him to change the machine. They wheeled in the third machine and gave me the news I never dreamt of hearing in a million years - the baby did not have a heartbeat. Not accepting or wanting to process the information, I demanded a c-section.

They told me I risked losing my life, but I said I didn't care. They moved me into the prep room to get ready for the operation, but within moments the baby came out in full force. Not feeling any pain, all I saw was my baby. She was sleeping, a full set of hair, chubby; a carbon copy of her older sister Simi. The doctors tried everything, but there was still no heartbeat. That was it. They took her away.

I demanded to know what had gone wrong. How had I lost my daughter when I just felt her moving, minutes ago. I did not want to conduct the funeral until I knew why she left us so soon, leaving footprints in our hearts. I remember ringing the hospital on the day of the funeral to find out if they had any reasoning for me. They told me there had been a placental eruption. "These just happen sometimes, when the placenta comes away from the wall..." "How?" I asked. "There is no given reason," they replied, "sometimes it just comes away."' This is the only explanation they could provide. They told me the UK has among the highest rate of stillborn babies in the whole of Europe, because we only have two check-ups here whereas elsewhere in Europe there is a scan every month. "It's just one of those things," the hospital said. But it's not just one of those things. "Mummy, where is the baby?" Simi would ask me. I told her that the baby wasn't well, and that she'd gone to her nana's (my dad's) house to be with her nana and my grandad, and they are all going to take care of each other. I invented a world for my children for people who pass away; I tell them they are all together and waiting for us, so my children don't feel people are gone and that there is another place for them to go.

We named her Riya. Mothers will do anything for their children, and I had to move forward because my eldest daughter and my husband needed me. It wasn't easy, to bear this loss. It shook my world. I couldn't believe it had been possible to lose a baby the way I lost Riya, and it took me nine months of suffering from insomnia, lying awake day and night, feeling I could see a baby standing by the door some nights, having no motivation or energy, before I could begin the healing process. I had to carry on for the sake of my family, and I put my grief aside to focus on what I had. I remember that the mums in Simi's nursery made a message book for me when I was recovering, and there were fifteen mothers from the same nursery who had all had miscarriages too. I thought, I go out with these people all the time and no one has mentioned what they had all been through - baby loss. It's still a taboo, women are suffering in silence. It doesn't seem right to me that so many women can suffer from the same problem which should not even be a problem, especially in England with all the facilities available. Funding issues within NHS and expertise is contributing to the high number of miscarriages women experience - change urgently needs to be made to prevent other women becoming part of the statistics.

When I was pregnant the third time with my son, we didn't tell my daughter until I was showing, and the first thing she said was: "Is the baby going to stay with us, or nana?" "Simi, this baby is going to stay with us," I told her. It was a very nervous pregnancy, there was not much excitement as the fear of losing the baby was there. Having endured the miscarriage previously this pregnancy was closely monitored and my consultant was an Indian doctor which I think really helped. He always made an extra effort to calm me down before my appointments as he knew my situation and knew there was a sense of anxiety. The baby was delivered with a planned c-section at 38 weeks.

Simi was not told about the delivery date, she was picked up from school and brought to the hospital thinking it was just a checkup but when she arrived, her face glowed. The joy on her face of seeing her baby brother was beautiful and I'll never forget her face and the excitement in her heart.

I want people to be able to talk about the struggles they go through, to know that they are not alone and that they don't have to deal with such difficult problems in silence. When I lost my baby, I reached out to the Stillborn and Neonatal Death Charity, Sands, but I found it hard to connect, purely because of the cultural differences. I felt that British and Asian culture and lifestyles were so different and I think this results in Asians shying away from the help available.

I am Heena, mother of three children.

Life isn't always straightforward or easy, stretching and pulling you in all directions, but we have to take a step back, analyse the situation and embrace it. Taboo subjects like baby loss only stay a taboo if we accept things the way they are.

Don't change yourself to be accepted, change the world to accept you: we have already made so much progress for the greater good.

CHAPTER 13

Accountancy to Accolades

NINA AMIN MBE

Nina Amin MBE was a partner and head of Asian Markets at KPMG until 31 January 2018. She is one of the founders of Unicorn Ascension Fund, a UK-based technology fund, and acts as the chair of its investment committee. She is a chartered accountant and over the lengthy span of her career has won many awards, confirming her at the peak of her industry. In 2013, she was awarded an MBE for services to the Asian business community and she also has a 2008 award for Professional of the Year, the 2009 Asian Who's Who Leadership award and the Woman of the Year award in 2017.

She is a board member of TiE London, a body that promotes entrepreneurship in the UK and was elected as President on 1 January 2018. She has recently been appointed to the Cancer Research UK Catalyst board and was until recently Vice Chair of the trustee board of Lepra. Nina shared her story of being a career woman and a mother with all the associated trials and tribulations. Her ambition and vision has paved the way for the next generation of professionals and entrepreneurs. I was truly inspired by her drive and passion.

*

Moving to London and becoming a chartered accountant was my goal from the age of thirteen. I grew up in Mombasa, Kenya with my parents and two sisters. In 1957, my parents embarked upon an uncertain new path sailing in a ship from India to Africa, a journey which took forty days, and 18 years later I wanted to continue our family journey by moving to England in search of better opportunity for myself and my family. In those days, it was really difficult, as my mum and dad were from modest backgrounds and sending me to London was very expensive. But my dad had unwavering faith in me and helped me through the entire process of getting my student visa and applying to colleges. My dad was very much a family man; he wanted his three daughters to succeed in life and wanted us to be independent at a time where independence and career aspirations were luxuries not afforded to most women. He was very keen for all of us to have a good education and professional qualifications. He is my inspiration, my hero, because if he hadn't believed in me and given me the opportunity to defy the stereotypical expectations of girls, I wouldn't be here today. I had big ambitions and he let me reach for them, while my mum supported our whole family with her unconditional love.

Leaving Kenya for London when I was seventeen was an immense culture shock for me. I could speak English, of course, but other than that, I didn't really appreciate English culture or its traditions. Food was a big issue because I was brought up as a vegetarian and was used to home cooked Gujarati food all the time - in 1975 London, you couldn't find any of the Indian food restaurants we have now. I was staying with a family as a paying guest and trying to respect their rules and regulations which was a big adjustment for me. Living in Mombasa, which was a small port, leading a sheltered life where my parents met all my needs, I knew very little about what was going on outside of Mombasa before I arrived in England.

While studying for A-Levels, I signed up for a one-year conversion course, after which you could go straight into a four-year training contract with a chartered accountant firm to qualify as an accountant. I sat down with the directory of all the accountancy firms in England and applied to around one hundred firms for a training contract. I didn't have a computer, we didn't have email, so I literally sat down and hand wrote hundreds of letters. Rejection after rejection flowed in. Nobody was willing to even consider an interview with me, let alone offer me a training contract. At that time, very few women went into the accountancy profession, and an Indian woman was unheard of. 'Oh my god, nobody is going to give me a job,' I thought.

Becoming an accountant was my dream, and I could see that even with my hard work, it was slipping away from me. Just as I was close to giving up, a friend of the family I was living with who worked as a chartered accountant said he would ask his boss if they had any training contracts available. He was working for a Jewish firm, and his boss called me in for an interview and offered me a training contract, which was conditional on me passing the conversion course. My starting salary was incredibly low, but I was so grateful to have any job that I signed the contract immediately.

I was the only woman studying the conversion course to get a training contract for the same firm. Competing with men, who all formed friendships with each other easily, was a difficult time for me as I felt so left out. When September came and our results from the conversion course were going to be published on a board at college, two guys from my course said they would go and find out if they had passed, and check if I had passed too. "'Nina, we looked at the pass list and we couldn't see your name, so we thought you had failed," they told me, "but then we looked at the fail list, and we couldn't see your name either." It turned out I was in the top ten list. Actually, I came second overall.

My colleagues' stereotypical expectations of me were shattered!

Part two of the exam for becoming a chartered accountant was even more difficult - only around twenty percent of people passed first time. In my mind, there was no way I could afford to fail the exam, I was so determined. Life is not easy - anything that is worth having will require exceptional hard work. We need to have clear goals about what we want and develop strategies about how we will achieve it. No matter how good your strategy is, you're going to have ups and downs because things never go according to plan. So, all I can say is never give up. If you fail, fine, but if you give up, that's the end of your journey. A strong will is the key to succeeding. Out of the seventeen people studying for the second exam at my firm, I was the only one who passed.

The partner who I was working for at the firm didn't even call me initially - he assumed I had failed. When he did call, I said: "Look, now that I'm fully qualified, can I get the fully qualified pay rate?" I'd worked so hard and knew this was exactly what I deserved. He told me he'd speak to the other partners, and the following day he told me I still had six months left on my training contract, so I had to wait six months to get full pay. I was so upset - everybody else had failed, so they would just be taking study leave and not doing their job for the next six months, whereas I had passed so would be working as a fully qualified accountant with much less pay than this work deserved. I decided to leave the firm when the training contract ended, and applied to the top eight accountancy firms in the UK at the time. I got offers from three and decided to take an offer from Arthur Andersen, who impressed me the most as they invested a whole day with me during the recruitment process and then couriered the job offer to me the following day.

Before I started at Arthur Andersen, I met my husband while doing final exams for chartered accountancy. He was also studying to be a chartered accountant, and we dated for three years before getting married in 1982. We are both from Gujarati backgrounds, but he comes from a different community to mine and we therefore had to convince our parents to let us get married. My husband and I are both Hindus, so we share many similar values and cultural traditions, but his Patel community and my Jain community work in different ways, and our extended families would have preferred us to marry within our communities, they thought it was not the done thing. However, they realised we wanted this and they loved us, saw everything we had in common, and saw how happy we made each other so they eventually came on board.

After we got married, we decided that we would wait a while before starting a family - we wanted to enjoy married life and to get our careers established and felt that doing so would be a lot easier if we didn't have children to take care of. Bringing a child into our lives was something we wanted when the timing was right.

My daughter was born when my husband and I had been married for six years, and we had my son two years after. At this point, I was director with a company called Chiltern Financial Services and was thriving in my career. I went back to work six months after my son was born, and so we had a full-time nanny to take care of him. Unfortunately, she had an accident and suddenly we were left without child support. I asked my mum and dad, who were living in Kenya at the time, if they would be able to look after my son. They were so happy to look after him, they flew to London and took him back to Kenya with them. He was a cute one year old, but I think he understood that he was with his parents one day, and the next day he wasn't. Even though my mum and dad looked after him incredibly well, I think he was shocked by the sudden change and being thousands of miles away without his mother, father, or sister. His milestones were delayed as a result, and by the time he was two, he was barely walking or talking. My mum advised me that I needed to take my son home to see a specialist to find out if anything was wrong. The doctor couldn't physically find anything wrong with him - at that point, my son just really needed his mother. I knew I had to hand in my notice at work.

"You're a director in the company, and we can't hold this position open indefinitely, so if you don't know when you are coming back, we have to replace you," my boss told me. I didn't care, and I told him there was nothing I could do about it. I took a career break for four years to get my son back on track. It was a really difficult and emotional time, especially when I used to take him to speech therapy, physiotherapy, and just generally dedicate a lot of time to looking after him and helping him to live a normal life. I think it paid off, because he eventually went to Oxford University and now works as a chartered accountant for KPMG. It was worth taking this time off to grow a strong bond with my son and give him the attention that he needed. My personal experience with my son has taught me that with love, care, attention, and the right guidance, you can help your children to unlock their full potential despite whatever difficulties they may be facing.

When my son had recovered and got into an outstanding school at age seven, I decided this was the time to go back to work. I was offered a job at KPMG, where I worked all the way back up to a director position for the second time. It was hard returning from a break, you get a bit rusty when you're out of the workplace for a long time, but I had my mind set on it. Not only did I want to get back into the working life, I wanted to make partner at KPMG. A key piece of advice I want to share is that having a sponsor helps to achieve ambitious goals like mine. A sponsor is the person who is going to help you get to where you want to be. At KPMG, I worked hard to sufficiently impress enough people at a senior level who knew me and believed in me, so that they were there to help me on my career path. We need mentors, people who support us and make us feel good with encouragement, but we also need sponsors: the people who are in the position of influence to make something happen for you. In 2004, after seven years with the firm my name was finally put forward for a partner position at KPMG.

Shortly after I was made partner, the head of my department asked if I would build up relationships with the Asian businesses in London as he felt that KPMG could add value to them. He knew there was a thriving Indian community in London and he wanted KPMG to become the preferred professional advisory firm for them and give them the best professional support. As a professional with technical expertise and practical experience in advising clients, thinking about how to build relationships from scratch and convince businesses to change their advisers to a large global (and let's be honest more expensive) firm, was a new type of skill for me. I decided the best way forward was to do a social event specific to the community, and to my relief, we had a great turnout, with eighty-five percent of the people we invited attending. Over time, this became a flagship annual event in the KPMG calendar and one of the most popular events that everyone wanted to attend. I was able to build a substantial Asian business network for KPMG. One of the MPs recognised my hard work and achievement of bringing people together, and put my name forward for an MBE, which I was awarded in 2013. An MBE stands for Member of the Most Excellent Order of the British Empire. It was an absolute honour and privilege to be recognised for my work.

As well as working for KPMG, I have also volunteered as a Vice Chair of the Trustee Board for the charity Lepra for seven years, and as an ambassador for the British Asian Trust for five years. With both roles, I decided to step down after being involved for a while because I think that with any organisation or role, there needs to be change and the opportunity for new people to establish new ideas. In 2018, when I turned sixty, I also decided to step down from KPMG, because I wanted to move on to other things. Since retiring, my life has changed a lot, and I've become president of TiE London, which is part of TiE Global, one of the largest not-for-profit organisation that promotes and fosters entrepreneurship in the UK. We are a membership organisation that offers mentorship, education, networking and we have an angel network that invests in start-ups and scaleups. We have networks for women and for young entrepreneurs and I launched the TiE Awards in 2018 where we recognise some of the top entrepreneurs in London.

I've recently been appointed on the Cancer Research UK Catalyst board. As one of the largest killers in the world, cancer research is a cause I am incredibly passionate about and having personally lost loved ones to cancer it is a cause very close to my heart. I am proud to be involved with such a reputable charity that does critical work in trying to improve the lives of patients with the disease as well as furthering our understanding of cancer so as a society we can improve the efficacy of treatment and hence survival rates.

Stepping down as Partner at KPMG also meant I could embark on my next career path in technology investment where I founded Unicorn Ascension Fund. So far, we've made seven investments into fast-growing companies with new technology, and the plan is to take these technologies to the rapidly-digitalising Indian market. We are focusing on disruptive technologies which will innovate the way businesses and organisations currently work, and we have a team in India looking into these technologies to see if they would work in India.

For three years running , my husband and I have been named one of the top 100 Asian Power Couples. One of the most important things to me is having a great support system in place, because you can't do it all on your own. I always say, surround yourself with people who are positive, who are there for both good times and bad times. We deserve people who support us unconditionally, even when things are difficult. When my husband and I visited his grandmother in Gujarat,

I realised the true importance of family, and respect for your family and your elders. Gujarat is so full of life and colour and an abundance of traditions - at the core of it all is community spirit. Perhaps sometimes I don't realise it, or actively miss it, but this is a part of me and I've been raised to have these cultural values and pay respect to your elders. I've taught my own children about how to pay respect to their grandparents and other elders when they see them. We live in a largely materialistic world and when you're chasing money and success, you can forget that actually, there are other things in life that are far more important than success and financial gain such as family, relationships and the important human qualities of kindness, compassion and community. And I think that Covid-19 has certainly taught us that!

On our visit to Gujarat, I remember sitting on the floor making chapatis with my husband's grandmother. She was in her nineties and lived alone in this tiny little house in a little village, where all of the neighbours knew that we were coming to visit so they came to greet us and were so happy to welcome us. I sat down with her on the floor of my grandma-in-law's kitchen to help her with the cooking - my chapatis were all over the place, but she didn't criticise me and neither did anyone else when we all ate as a family. We connected by spending that time together cooking, reminding me that the most valuable part of life is the love, respect, and the connections we can share with others.

CHAPTER 14

Dharmic Life

TRUPTI PATEL

Trupti Patel is a civil engineer, the first female president of the Hindu Forum of Britain, and the former first female chair of the north-western branch of Chartered Institute of Highways and Transportation. She is also the former president of the Hindu Council of the North, a dance guru and teacher who organised a group of over 300 community members to perform at the 2002 Commonwealth Games closing ceremony. After graduating from the forward-thinking university town of Vallabh Vidyanagar, in Gujarat, and moving to England at the age of twenty-one, Trupti encountered many unexpected prejudices as an intelligent young Indian engineer; we spoke about how persistence and self-belief are vital in the face of adversity. Trupti is an incredibly talented woman with a beautiful philosophy about how we can live a fulfilled life without expecting any rewards. She actively campaigns to improve inclusivity for the Hindu community in the United Kingdom.

*

When I was fifteen, India still had a system of supporting small businesses through a barter system where exchange of commodities was normal; I met a poor young mother whose only way of making a living for herself and her tiny baby was by trading new pots and pans for old saris and clothes. These women have almost nothing; every day they walk from door to door and people would invite them into their homes and offer old items in exchange for the pots. The young mother I met had been accused of stealing someone's saris. Prison sentences were incredibly long for petty crimes at the time, so this one accusation had the potential to ruin this woman's life. However, my mentor at the time, an amazing woman who worked on reform plans in womens' prisons and on improving the terrible conditions female inmates experienced, took up the poor woman's case and helped her get out of jail. My mentor, Ms Hemlataben Hegiste, one of the pillars of the Sameetee in Gujarat, helped these women reform their lives and devoted her time to providing them with support – she taught me that if someone has a problem, we can try to understand why, and support them in moving forward. We should never judge people just by looking at them, and we should help those in need without expecting anything in return.

On the one hand, women were respected immensely as teachers and professors at the Sardar Patel University and on the other, watching such injustices happening to women from disadvantaged communities – as I was growing up – made me incredibly headstrong about speaking out against inequality. As the first female president of the Hindu Forum of Britain (HFB), I am highly focused on campaigning for integration, interfaith communication, and correct usage of religious symbols in England. The HFB allows us to have a voice as a community to express any concerns we have with government matters; it is this voice which means we can work towards the acceptance and understanding of Indian culture in the UK. We are a tolerant group of people; I believe we are taken for granted in this country, and now is the time for us to stand up for ourselves.

As a volunteer and representative for Indian origin people of Hindu faith in the UK, I lead my life by the same Dharmic principles which my mentor followed, in order to provide for others without expecting any personal gain. Dharma is not attached to one religion in India: for example you could be Hindu, Sikh, Jain or Buddhist. The concepts are rather attached to a way of life which could be adopted by anyone: being a good Dharmic person means striving to be virtuous and honest, and volunteering without wanting to receive anything in return.

When I was growing up in India, my father also held Dharmic values, and always encouraged my brothers and I to be caring and respectful to everyone around us. My father was an English professor at Sardar Patel

University, and he used to give free English lessons to the children in our town, regardless of their background, because he focused on giving without judgement. He saw that everyone needed to learn English, and that everyone should be able to learn even if they can't afford to pay. Growing up at the Sardar Patel University, my brothers and I were raised in a stimulating, intellectual, university town, filled with art, sports, and culture. We learnt that it didn't matter what status you had in the university, from the professors to the deans to the caretaker's children or the cleaners, everybody worked just as hard. All of us children played together and studied together, undivided, and looking back on it now, at our country which British imperialists attempted to divide, it was truly powerful that we kept this notion that we were all equal.

The imperialist division in India by the British, which I am referring to, is the creation of the caste system. I believe the caste system was directly caused by European and in particular Portuguese imperialism: When the British were ruling India, they separated society into rigid classes, because the division of people meant it was far easier for Britain to rule over everyone in the country. When colonialisation started in India, it was difficult for Britain to understand a country so different from their own carefully constructed society and dividing Indian people into castes making the process of imperialism easier. But India suffered and still suffers massively from this introduction of a complete caste system, and there is considerable prejudice against those in lower strata of society.

From the HFB we led one of the most important fights to prevent the caste system issue from prevailing in the UK. A caste clause was put into Equality Law to help prevent caste-based discrimination, but we deeply feel this is inappropriate – the equality law states that we are all equal, so why single out Hindu society by making a separate clause about caste? If everyone is equal, it is not necessary to add new legislation regarding an outdated system which was introduced during the colonialisation process to harm Indian society. We have fought tooth and nail against a separate caste clause because we do not want to be separated in legislation from others – we want to share the same notion of equality for everyone. I want our Indian community to feel like an important part of the United Kingdom and to be accepted as equal.

My strong focus on community and inclusivity stems from my university town upbringing: including everyone's status wasn't a question in our town, and my father always encouraged me to work hard for whatever I wanted. I was lucky enough to study civil engineering at the same university where my father taught. The creation of Sardar Patel University was highly influenced by Sardar Vallabh bhai Patel himself – during India's independence movement, Patel saw the need for higher education in more places around India so that there could be education of people locally in India everywhere, instead of all students being localised in bigger cities. I began studying Engineering at Birla Vishwakarma Mahavidyala and graduated from the Engineering College in 1972 having completed my degree in civil engineering by age twenty-one. On our course, we would begin workshops early at seven o'clock in the morning and wouldn't finish lectures until five o'clock in the evening – we worked hard, and were extremely busy. I was one of only a handful of girls doing an engineering degree, so there was a lot of adoration from the boys on our course. We'd get proposals and all sorts, but it was all entertaining and we had a lot of fun together. Mini-skirts and short dresses were very popular at the time, and we'd leave the house wearing whatever we wanted and bring along a huge handkerchief to cover our legs while sitting down! It was an amazing time; our modern university town really made us feel like we could achieve anything – many of the civil engineers from my university have gone on to accomplish great things. I learned that I could do anything I wanted as a strong, young Indian woman with a Hindu identity - a lesson which proved invaluable when I moved to England shortly after graduating.

I had never really considered how women could be pushed aside in the workplace purely based on their gender until I came to England with a high-standard degree in civil engineering and was offered only secretarial work. Straight after finishing university, I got married and me and my husband Jagdish (who had been on my engineering course with me) moved to London because his family came in 1972 driven away from Uganda and settled in Ealing. My father in-law took us to a job centre and the woman behind the desk could not understand that I didn't want to do a secretarial job: "Girls always do secretarial jobs,"' she told me, "I can find you one easily." But I refused – I could not let all of my hard work be for nothing. The black-and-white boundaries about what women were considered incapable of doing just because they were women enraged me: actively discouraging women from taking on any type of position in the workplace is detrimental for everybody in society. When my brothers and I were in our teens, our mother studied for her BA in Sanskrit and Statistics and then completed her MA in Statistics, showing us all that a woman can do anything she wanted to and embark on ambitious career paths, even after having three children. I am her very proud daughter, and as I applied for jobs, my mother's achievements served as a constant reminder that there were no limitations for what I could achieve just because I was a woman. With all of my determination and six months of searching, I began my first civil engineering job at London Borough of Ealing in Technical Services.

The difficulties of adjusting to life in seventies England were far from over – nobody expected, or even considered, that an Indian girl who came from a small university town in the middle of nowhere could be highly capable as an engineer. Offices at the time were predominantly made up of white employees, I was one of the only females of colour in Technical Services, and people would automatically assume I was someone's personal assistant. People constantly underestimated me. They were also unfortunately very ignorant about Indian culture; I remember one day when a man in our office turned to me and said: "Trupti, tell me something, when did you find time to study engineering while you were picking the tea leaves?"

"What do you mean?" I replied.

"My uncle told me that every woman in India has to learn how to pick tea leaves, how to brew tea, and how to resist burning their hands."

I was amazed by his pure obliviousness as to how offensive this was, and he went on to tell me he thought all Indian women have to die with their husbands. Racist ignorant remarks such as this were not scrutinised or discouraged in the UK in the seventies, in fact, I think racism was at its worst with a lot of people making no effort to be politically correct or supportive of other cultures in the UK – especially of cultures which are a part of the UK as a result of British imperialism. People had ridiculous and harmful preconceptions about the other communities living in the UK. I think the older generation, myself included, thought that since we were in a foreign land we should just accept the ignorant remarks with a pinch of salt and get on with our work. As a young woman, I accepted that I wasn't going to be understood and tried to focus on the work in front of me to make them aware of our culture by contributing in small ways on BBC channels and other mediums. After some time, I said to myself: "I think it's time to stand up for what we deserve: we are a valid part of British community life, and negative preconceptions about our ethnicity should not be allowed to stand!"

One ray of positivity that did shine through when I worked at various engineering jobs was that a lot of people from Asian backgrounds were able to see me as a friendly face and ask me for help. People would ask me, perhaps in Punjabi, Gujarati, Hindi or Urdu, all of which I understand, if I could help them to navigate through the maze of Local Government regulations and procedures. Overall, in London there was this sense of community spirit amongst people with a background from the Indian subcontinent.

Despite the discrimination I experienced as a young Indian civil engineer in the seventies, I continued to rise up in my career and took up the position of a group engineer at the Three Rivers District Council in Hertfordshire. My husband and I both decided we wanted to get our Master's degrees, and I completed mine in Highways and Transportation from City University, London. Shortly afterwards, I began working for Manchester City Council as the lead group engineer, and I had three different teams working for me. I think the older generation of workers, predominantly white workers, did not like working under a woman from an ethnic minority background. However, at that time in 1994, I was the highest-ranking local government officer of Indian origin in the UK. In 2000 I moved to Salford City Council as a group engineer first and rose to become Acting Associate Director of the Traffic and Transportation Division and in 2005 appointed as the 'Traffic Manager (Network)' under Traffic Management Act 2004 - first female engineer to hold the post. Even though perhaps the councillors sometimes didn't like the advice I gave, I stood my ground, believed in myself, and focused on what was important: balancing everyone's needs in the community. For example, if you are looking at a planning application for the Media City Lowry, Salford Quays, you have to look at the whole site and think through all of these questions: What kind of traffic will this generate? What kind of pedestrian movement will it generate? What infrastructure do you need to provide, such as accessible facilities for all and improvement in the area? Every new development is one piece of the jigsaw which creates the entire town, and one small change will affect everything. When I looked at every planning application, I would think, yes, so we are generating all of these things, now what are we giving back to the community? I would present a win-win situation – showing the councillors how it will be beneficial to them, and how it is giving back to the community. I always worked on bringing people together and building the infrastructure that fit well for the community needs.

While I was working as acting associate Director of the Traffic and Transportation Division for Salford City council, I also started a supplementary dance school called 'Nrtya Jyoti' at the Indian Association Oldham in Greater Manchester, which was an amazing period of my life. Six of us women started with a mothers' and daughters' group, teaching them dances. During the Commonwealth games in 2002, I trained nearly three hundred women and children, both boys and girls, to participate with me in the closing ceremony. I loved teaching dance, and my students would travel with me all around Europe to dance in different festivals. The Lowry in Manchester, a fantastic theatre that hosts dances and plays, became like a second home; we would organise competitions and events all the time. Children who enjoy what they're doing will perform better in school, so being able to join in with the dancing school made a big difference.

Volunteering with the dance school reminded me and the children I worked with that studying isn't everything; it's so important to live a well-rounded life filled with experiences you're passionate about. I am extremely grateful I could give back to the community as a dance teacher, as well as campaigning in the Hindu community. Inspired by my father, my Dharmic philosophy means I focus on searching for ways to self-improve, accepting everyone regardless of their background, and providing help where help is needed without expecting rewards. With my position as the president of the HFB, I want to ensure that we look for ways to elevate our own community in the UK, and ensure we prevent any unfair legislation or events taking place which will cause difficulties for us and for future generations. It has also taken time for the HFB to become a place which is representative of all who are part of our culture, and we have worked hard to make this happen. I am really proud of the initiative that the HFB led and set up in 2020 with their strategic team called HEART - Hindu Emergency Action Response Team, inviting all major national organisations; HSS, NCHT, HCUK and VHP along with BAPS. For the first time ever we all worked together to combat the ill effects of the Covid-19 Pandemic.

Our whole world is one beautiful tapestry, and it is our responsibility to make sure that we are all woven together in the threads; if there's a problem in the making of the tapestry, you have to work out what's wrong. If there are traditions in our community which are not conducive to the well-being of the community, we have to move forward – we have to approach ourselves and our community constructively and improve ourselves before improving the environment around us.

CHAPTER 15

Defining Moment

VARSHA MISTRY

Varsha Mistry has been serving with the Metropolitan police for over thirty-six years. She is now a forensic practitioner who specialises in detecting and recovering fingerprint evidence. As an immigrant from Zambia with Gujarati heritage, who was the only woman of colour at her police station when first posted as a crime scene examiner in the 1980s, Varsha shared with me the difficulties she has encountered in England. She also told me about the great strides towards inclusivity in the police service, some of which she has helped to make. Ever since a near-death experience irrevocably changed her life, Varsha has volunteered on different projects, including as the first female chairperson for the Met Police Hindu Association, and as regional director of Hindu Council UK. With a brilliant perspective regarding how we should give back without expecting anything in return, and with great focus on how we can work within our communities to achieve change, Varshas' attitude is inspiring. She follows a Hindu ethos of a non-harmful existence and is a calm and gentle person - but she is also driven, focused, and powerfully ambitious about taking the steps in her power to improve different situations within her community and to support the people around her.

*

Everything changed in just one moment. My husband was driving my children and myself home from a wedding when our car skidded out of control. It veered backwards across all three lanes of the motorway, hit the central reservation, and then rolled over two and a half times with all of us in it. When the car stopped on its side, it felt like everything in the world stopped. All I could think was: "Where's my baby? Is my baby okay?" My son was just a few months old. I reached to the baby seat next to me to touch him and he was not there. During the crash, my head must have banged against the car and now my mind was spinning. Slowly, I looked around and saw that the roof was completely crunched inwards and I was told there was petrol leaking out of the car. Within minutes, people started appearing and helping to lift my children and us out after breaking a window as the best exit from the car. "You must get out, you need to get out!" They were saying repeatedly. I could not think, I could not focus on anything. My two young daughters got out first, then my husband and I was stuck in the bottom side of the car. When I was lifted out, I saw my husband and his arm was completely ripped to bits and broken in several places. "Where's my baby? Where's my baby?" I kept on saying, and then I saw him: covered in a blanket being fed by a stranger who had stopped to help, completely fine. He did not have a single scratch on him. My two young daughters were sitting on the grass verge wrapped in blankets and they too were fine.

My precious family was almost ripped away from me in less than a minute, but here they were, still in front of me, still safe.

I think I was quite hedonistic before the car crash. I used to be relatively shallow, but after thinking I lost my whole family, what was truly important came into focus – I was so grateful we were alive; we were lucky enough to survive this horrible accident and I was incredibly appreciative to the emergency services and ordinary people who selflessly stopped to help us. From that day forward I have focused on how I could give back. When the accident happened, I was on maternity leave from my job in the Metropolitan Police Service. I have always enjoyed my job – especially examining crime scene evidence and therefore helping to find justice for victims – but when I went back to work later that year in 2003, I knew I also wanted to devote more time to helping the community. Everyone had helped my family so much when we were recovering from the accident – I wasn't able to drive due to an injury on my spine, so friends and family took turns driving my children to school. My husband's arm injury also meant he could not work for six months, and as I was then on unpaid maternity leave with our new son, we were about to face nearly six months without income. An act of pure kindness saved us from this tough situation: my husband's friend, soon after the accident, came over to our house and gave us an envelope for our bills. He supported us until my husband could go back to work – his generosity and huge heart has been so important to our family, and truly inspired me to do whatever I could to help others when I recovered.

Upon my return to work, I saw an email about the Met Police Hindu Association, which was recently formed. I decided that, despite having three young children, I wanted to try and help as much as I could and I began volunteering at different events at New Scotland Yard and in the community. I was then asked to join the committee, and I began doing a huge amount of voluntary work. I found it was a lovely and essential channel for giving back. For four years, I served as the first female chairperson of the Met Police Hindu Association – during this time, I helped voluntarily with police recruitment, crime prevention initiatives, community engagement and fundraising projects. Volunteering for the association helped me and others to understand more about Indian history and the Hindu faith. Hinduism is one of the oldest religions – we believe everybody is connected by their souls and all form part of one great soul connecting us to the almighty. This means that if I give you something, I don't expect a thank you as I'll only be helping myself, because we are always connected by this greater soul and therefore we embrace humanity in its entirety as one family. The religious presentations and workshops during the MPHA events enriched my outlook on life and helped me to become a person who looks beyond herself and thinks about what one can do for others.

I believe these volunteering endeavours have helped me to gain a far better understanding of how the Hindu faith has given my parents such strong resilience. My mother and father are both from Surat, in Gujarat, India, but for the first three and a half years of my life we lived in Kenya and then Zambia. Life was beautiful in Zambia – we had a bungalow with fresh fruits and vegetables growing in the garden, and my mum would cook fresh food for my three siblings and me, and a Gujarati and African community surrounded us. My dad's strength as I grew up was indefatigable: he was the sole supporter for his sister (until she got married) and parents as well as his own family of six and he was always ready to provide whatever was needed for us and support his friends and wider family. When I was three and a half years old and my father moved us to

England in the hope of finding a more reliable income to support us all, his patience and resilience only became more powerful. England in the seventies was not a welcoming place for immigrants. In Zambia, my dad had been an accounts clerk but here in England he was turned away from white collar jobs, even with all of his experience. Eventually, he became a bus conductor – he used to take a lot of abuse in this job from racist people who travelled on the bus. Both of my parents faced intolerant attitudes of people with racial prejudices when they moved to England, but they never complained. We were living in a time when shops had signs saying: 'No blacks or dogs.' However, my parents never reacted negatively and always stayed calm – they somehow learned to shrug it off and ignore it. My parents' strength, and their ability to remain giving, loving, and caring people who go out of their way to help others, even after experiencing such hostility when they arrived here, is exactly what I strive towards.

The difficulties we experienced as a family when we moved to England extended to my school life. I was terrified when I first began school; I only spoke Gujarati and some Kiswahili. At school, everything was so different to what I was used to. In Zambia we had experienced a welcoming and comfortable community and the routine traditions of my parents' Gujarati heritage – everyone eating together, enjoying group gatherings. These had always been, and of course still are, an integral part of our daily lives. However, in my new school in England, I was suddenly isolated. There were not many other people of colour, and girls who lived near us and would talk to me outside of school now ignored me during lessons and the playground. "It's okay to play with you outside school, but not at school," I recall one of the girls telling me. Other children were uncomfortable to be around me and kept their distance from me. I didn't understand why; I couldn't understand my new environment. It was a very lonely time.

I think that slowly, things are changing in England, and with pro-active people fighting for what they believe in, our country can become a more accepting and inclusive place for everyone. Though it was hard when I was a child, now, I have the strength to question why things are the way they are and to work towards exactly what is necessary to make change. For some issues, we have even gone as far to lobby our local MP in order to draw attention to inequalities. It wasn't right that people treated me differently because I came from a different culture, but when you are an immigrant in the country, when you feel like you are a guest, albeit an unwanted guest, you are far less likely to criticise or protest your maltreatment. However, I have pride in my heritage. Indian history is not taught well in British schools, but when I learned our history on my own accord, and understood how important India has been to the British economy for over 200 years, and how much our Indian forefathers have given to this country, including millions giving their lives during both World Wars to support Britain, I learned to be more confident of my place here and proud of my attributes. I encourage everyone to stand with pride no matter where they are from, and realise their place is valid. The drive for change is most powerful when you stand with confidence and certainty that you deserve to be a valued part of your country.

Change happens when passionate people work together – the reason I volunteer on committees in the police force and beyond is to help the job and wider society become an inclusive and fair place for everyone. I first joined the Met Police Service aged seventeen. At the time, I didn't really know much about which career direction I wanted to go in, but almost all of the Asian ladies who I knew mainly worked in shops, factories, banks or in other office jobs. I didn't feel enthused about these and that would have been the wrong path for me. A job with the Met police appealed to me, so I applied and began working in the fingerprint department at New Scotland Yard in 1983. While working here, I finished my A-levels at college, and thereafter applied to become a fingerprint expert. I trained for five years – I worked with various aspects of fingerprint coding, classifications, examinations, comparisons, chemical treatments, the recovery of fingerprints from cadavers, and crime scene examinations. After becoming the first Indian female to achieve Fingerprint Expert status in the Met Police, I was posted out to examine crime scenes for evidence recovery. At the time, the Met Police service was quite male-dominated. On my first scene examiner posting I was not only one of only a few women in the station, but I was the only person of colour in the whole building. When I first introduced myself to the detective chief inspector, he was very surprised to have a female crime scene examiner for the first time. This surprise extended to victims whose crime scenes I would examine. 'I expected a grey-haired man in a suit!' people would exclaim when they saw me. I would have to reassure these victims, that we are all trained in exactly the same way. As the only Hindu female working in the department when I started as a young woman, the job came with many challenges, however, by enhancing understanding amongst my colleagues and as a result of the work of the Met Police Hindu Association, we have made extremely beneficial changes now. We have ensured that in-house vegetarian catering suitable for people of the Hindu faith is provided, and that the dress code for our religion is accepted as a part of uniform in the Met Police. This inclusivity allows for many potential applicants, new members, and long-standing members of the police service who are not from white backgrounds to feel accepted and comfortable in their workplace.

As a committee, we felt that an essential reason for including Hindu dress code in the police is that we want the Met police to look and feel like London; London is rich with diverse cultures, and these cultures need to be represented in our public services. I think that in policing, it is incredibly beneficial to have people from all different backgrounds. Victims and potential new recruits often feel more comfortable talking to someone who they think may be from a similar background to themselves: perhaps, for example, community members of Hindu origin may find it easier to talk to an officer who they see wearing Hindu symbols as part of their uniform and with the potential added benefit of being able to communicate in an Indic language.

Speaking with victims has been an extremely important part of my job. When I first began examining different crime scenes independently after completing the required training, it felt quite overwhelming. Attending crime scenes as part of the daily routine involved meeting victims of crime and sadly on occasion becoming involved with recovery of evidence for those victims who had lost their lives. Victims of crime can be incredibly distressed and often need support. At times, even when I knew there was no forensic evidence at a burglary scene, I would stay with victims for an hour or so to help them calm down and tidy things up. Being the victim of a crime can be an awful shock, and I would often find out that elderly victims had passed on a month or two after the crime because the shock of a crime had caused detrimental impact on their health. I have worked for the Met Police for thirty-seven years now, and from the day that I started as a fingerprint officer there has always been an overwhelming sense of satisfaction to think that I could help to remove people from society who were causing harm. I feel happy to help deliver justice for the victims; I have spoken to thousands of victims and seen their distress, so to know I have helped them is a great achievement.

It is a privilege to serve with the Met Police towards delivering justice and creating a safer London. I now work in the Met Police Fingerprint Enhancement Laboratory. This entails working with a biology and trace scientists to try to recover all possible evidence such as DNA, hairs, fibres and fingerprints from an exhibit, which could be, for example, a knife or gun involved in a murder. Dressed in laboratory coats, gloves, masks and hair coverings, deciding a strategy together with our Biology and Trace team on how best to recover all evidence, we start with a series of different light source examinations – Ultra Violet, laser, blue crime lights, and different types of white lights are all used to try to detect fingerprints and other evidence. If there are any marks, we have them photographed immediately. To further visualise fingerprints, we sequentially use different chemicals and processing equipment to bring about a reaction to the various constituents found in human sweat or body fluids and relevant corrosion, which may be on the exhibit.

Successfully identifying someone for the crime they have committed is a truly amazing feeling even after thirty-seven years in the profession.

As well as my work in the lab, I have also been involved in the examination of serious crime, murder, counter-terrorism crime scenes and vehicles.

At one arson crime scene I visited, there were two young children sitting on the doorstep waiting for their grandmother to pick them up. As I went in to examine the premises, a friend of the children walked by and, shocked by the fire damage, asked about what had happened to the house, which had burnt down, and enquired where they were now going to live. The young girl responded, with complete normality, that her mum would have to go back to prison, and that she was lucky because she could live with her grandmother but that her brother was going to have to go back into care. The young girl spoke as if this was absolutely normal – for her, this was normal life. Hearing this reminded me how fortunate I am to have such stable support networks for my family, and to never take for granted the people who have helped me, or who would help me in a second if I needed it. This experience has also made me become a keen supporter of children's charities. My key focus at the moment is my children, who are in late education and starting to work now, and I want to ensure they understand how fortunate we are, and that they pay attention to the ways they can provide help to others. The community I was raised into and that my children have been raised into is one of total care and support, and I am endlessly grateful for this.

My parents, and their unlimited kindness and compassion for community, are my inspiration. When they finally bought their own house while I was growing up, we had rented a room to a young single gentleman. Eventually, he brought over his family of five siblings and parents from Kenya to stay with us. The mother, who was also of Gujarati origin, did not speak a word of English – I thought she was amazing, and I learnt so much from her. The family's plan was to stay with us for a short time until they found their own home, but tragically, the father was admitted to hospital with terminal lung cancer and died very shortly after his family moved to England. After this, the family ended up staying with us for much, much longer than expected – in our three bedroom and two-reception room house, there was my family of six with four children and then also the five additional children and their mother. To this day, even though this family now live in USA, they are still like our extended family, and it was brilliant that we could all come together and that my parents could provide support when it was most needed. Gujarati communities are often close-knit and ensure they are available to help each other. From this community spirit, I have learned that building a network of people, whether it's in your workplace, home life, or any other endeavour you may have, having people who you can rely on and who can rely on you is essential for success in life. It is much easier to overcome obstacles if you have others helping you and fighting for the same cause alongside you.

I am always inspired by my mother's achievements: she left her home in a village called Karan at sixteen and has since lived in five different countries, raised four children, and taught herself to speak English and Kiswahili. Everything I know about diplomacy I have learned from her – she is always great at keeping the peace and bringing everyone together. Both of my parents live a life of *ahimsa*, a non-harmful existence, and inspired by them I am also now vegan, focused on ways to stay healthy, and always trying to stay aware of how fortunate we are. At the same time, I am also passionate about driving change and achieving equality: questioning the status quo and changing unjustifiable situations is important. Don't sit down and accept things the way they are if you feel the situation is inexcusable. Take hold of what you believe in, work out the steps you need to take to do something about it, and do everything in your power to make it happen.

CHAPTER 16

Spinning Plates

HEERAL SHAH

Heeral Shah is the Head of UK Debt Structuring, Global Lending Group, Corporate Banking at Barclays Bank. She joined Barclays after graduating with a degree in Banking and International Finance from Cass Business

School, City University London in 1999. In our interview not only did we discuss how to be motivated at work, but also the importance of family and giving back to the community. Whilst life is a constant juggling game between competing priorities, it is important to ensure that everything starts with self-care and extends into taking joy in caring for others. As Heeral reminded me, even when life is jam-packed, we all deserve some time to focus on ourselves.

*

I have always been ambitious, striving to grow and become a better version of myself. At times, it was through leveraging some natural advantages - I was not the best at sport, but being tall helped me to make an impact: for example, in the netball team. Academic achievements did not come to me naturally, but I overcame that with a strong work ethic and determination to succeed. I went to school at the age of five, not speaking a word of English, but by my teens, I was a linguist at heart, with a passion for modern languages, Latin and classical studies. At the time, languages were perhaps not considered the pathway to a successful career and so I was guided to more traditional subjects like maths and economics. The inflection point came when I secured a place on the Windsor Fellowship programme at university, which opened the gateway to a sponsored internship with Barclays in 1998. This ultimately led to me joining the 1999 cohort of the Barclays Leadership Programme as one of only two Asian women. And so, my journey began.

I strongly believe my generation stands on the shoulders of giants – our grandparents and parents who travelled great distances with very little and sacrificed so much in an effort to provide their children with a better life. I am truly blessed to have parents who although they arrived in the UK with very little, strived and succeeded to provide me and my siblings with the best opportunities in life. My father had dreamt of becoming a pilot - a dream he could not fulfil as he had to turn his attention to securing a source of income. His strong maths skills and business acumen led him to a career in accountancy where through determination and hard work he secured a role at Arthur Andersen, where he specialised in Tax. Whilst on a strong career path, one that I have aspired to follow, my father's heart was also pulling him to maintain a balance between work, family and community. Frequently as a child, I would wake up in the early hours of the morning to find both my parents sitting at the dining table, still working as they strived to build their own business. The desire of independence and flexibility that running his own business would allow, encouraged my father to work harder to achieve this. Ultimately fulfilling his wish to dedicate more time to the family as well as carrying on with his community work, which was so important to him. This led to him setting up his own accountancy practice, which he is still leading today.

Education has always been a focus within the entrepreneurial and hard-working Gujarati community, and has been particularly important for my immediate family. At a time when it was not so common for the Indian community to consider independent schooling, my parents sought the best education and made the necessary sacrifices to allow my siblings and I to attend leading independent schools in Surrey. I aimed for no less than straight As when it came to my GCSE and A-Level exams and worked single-mindedly to do so. This displayed early evidence that my parents' and their community ethic had been engraved into my heart. I went on to read for a BSc. Banking and International Finance (Hons.) at the Cass Business School, City University London.

The world of banking and finance is incredibly fast-paced, innovative and people-focussed. As a natural introvert in my younger years, I had to push myself outside of my comfort zone every single day. Historically, financial services was a sector that did not really understand or promote cultural or gender diversity, equity and inclusion. Not that I thought about it at the time, there were many occasions in my early career where I was the only female or Asian person in the room. Needless to say, I have witnessed more junior and less qualified male colleagues being promoted or picked for a project ahead of me. Did I feel I had to work harder than others to get the same results? Absolutely! Did that drive me forward? Again, absolutely! Furthermore, as a female also wanting to have a family, there have inevitably been breaks from work, which did lead to questions about my commitment to my career in the long-term.

However, as a dedicated and ambitious female, I was determined to challenge the status quo. As I started to achieve more seniority at Barclays and take on more prominent roles within the organisation, I wanted to use my voice at the table to shape not just my own career, but also to influence those of the many colleagues taking a similar journey behind me. Witnessing the huge strides made to promote equality and support for gender and LGBTQ+ communities in our broader society, I realised there was more that the organisation could do to support ethnic minority colleagues. As the Windsor Fellowship programme opened the door for me to an institution that, as a young Asian female may not have been a natural fit, in turn, I have used my influence to guide and support many students who may not have ordinarily considered a career in banking and finance, let alone a university education. I have supported others through sponsoring a number of work experience programmes. It has been extremely rewarding to see those talented individuals return to join our internship or graduate programme.

In 2017, I founded the Asian Professionals Forum, which is part of Embrace, the multicultural network at Barclays. The objective remains: to support Asian colleagues through career progression, access to senior leaders and showcasing role models. Since launch, we have worked hard at breaking down some of the barriers that exist in large organisations by educating, leading and influencing change from the top, to help mould an organisation where all colleagues have the same opportunities and tools to succeed. With the more recent Black Lives Matter movement and as a member of the Race at Work taskforce, I have led this agenda for the Corporate Bank, focussed on stepping up our efforts to attract, develop, advance and retain Black as well as Asian and ethnically diverse professionals.

One of the most important lessons I have learnt in life is the need to build, nurture and invest in my network. This is something I have seen my father demonstrate - a super social networker who has an incredible ability to develop relationships with people from all walks of life. He is always willing to help others, be it with financial advice, connections or simply inviting a family who have recently arrived in the UK over for a home cooked meal. He has the ability to bring out the best in anyone, making them feel like the most important person in the room. His charming personality inspires me every day.

I also believe that actively managing your career is important. I have been fortunate to have some inspirational line managers, mentors, sponsors and coaches who have helped me to navigate and accelerate my career. It is important to seek independent advice from senior people, to be able to bounce ideas around and by trust and mutual respect for one another, to secure their support and guidance. They have continually encouraged me to review my three- and five-year plans, goals and aspirations. Of course there have been times when I haven't got this right, and encountered barriers along my career path, but with the support of my mentors and sponsors (both internal and external to the organisation), I have been able to continue to progress.

Dedicating so much time to your career can sometimes feel like you are married to your job and if you are not careful, it can negatively impact family life. I am a senior leader at Barclays, but I am also a wife, mother, sister, daughter and community member and maintaining balance in all aspects of one's life is a key part of the Gujarati value system. This is an innate virtue I have learnt from my own mother, who has also had a significant impact on my world outlook. My mother is the pillar in our family, forever supporting and giving, not only to those in her household, but to many others in the community too. Grounded in her religious beliefs, my mother emulates the values of leading a fulfilled life. Success is not measured solely through material means but also through spirituality. I want to be a similar role model; someone that my younger siblings and children can look up to as a tangible example of succeeding in all aspects of life. In order to do so, I have learnt that creating and prioritising time for those you love is incredibly important.

My parents always encouraged me to aim for the sky and to grab every opportunity. They advocated equality and never treated me differently to the boys in our extended family. With our own son and daughter, my husband Vishal and I guide them so they grow up knowing there are no limits to what they can achieve. We also make it a priority to instil in them the Gujarati values we have grown up with - be it praying together and fondly remembering our ancestors, sharing meals as a family without other distractions, or just being grateful for what we have in life.

My commitment to family time stems from the Gujarati values and deep religious beliefs with which I was raised. I was always surrounded by grandparents, cousins, aunts and uncles, with endless supplies of home-cooked food (we never had takeaways back in the day!) My kaka (dad's older brother) and his family lived with us for a year when they moved from Nairobi, before ultimately moving to the house next door and we always had our evening meal together. Even as an only child until the age of 11, I was never at home on my own! I always had my cousins and grandparents with me. For every celebration and family gathering, we would get together at my nani and nana's (maternal grandparents) or dadi and dada's (paternal grandparents). I will never forget the kindness with which my nani raised us. She would always say: "It doesn't matter who comes through your front door. Any visitor, any person who arrives at your door, is a form of God, and it is your duty to be kind to them, always offer a meal." If she heard of a friend or relative in hospital she would send my nana to deliver a delicious home cooked meal.

I am a big foodie and growing up in a Gujarati home in London meant I had access to great food. Not only do I love to cook and feed my family, I also love entertaining extended family and friends. The medicinal qualities of our Gujarati diet is something to celebrate. Dishes use fresh, healthy ingredients filled with nutrients that are incredibly beneficial to the body. Ginger, turmeric, black pepper, garlic, and chillies are just some of the spices used every day that help boost the immune system, enhance digestion, and build strength. A traditional Gujarati diet can make a huge difference to how your body and mind feel; when we share these meals together as a family or with friends, I believe that both our minds and bodies are nourished.

My parents are both the youngest of six siblings respectively, so my extended family is *huge* and I love the closeness we share. For me, my family always comes first. I have also married into a large Gujarati family with very similar beliefs and values. Soon after Vishal and I were engaged, we discussed moving back to the Midlands to support and live with his mother (my father-in-law had passed away some years earlier). I didn't question it. Having grown up in an extended family myself, I knew it was our duty. I was fortunate that I was able to transfer across to the same team within Barclays in Birmingham and continued to focus on my career, whilst settling into a new city, making new friends and getting to know my new family.

When I had both my children, on each occasion my mother and mother-in-law moved in with us to look after me, my husband and our new-born. I was lucky to have the support of my wider family and this environment had a hugely positive effect on my children, as they were pampered with ayurvedic massages and cuddles, and they were able to benefit from the best version of me, as I felt supported through what can be an exciting yet overwhelmingly emotional time. My mother-in-law is traditional yet fiercely independent and forward thinking, and only a few guests were allowed to visit the babies for five to six weeks, which meant we enjoyed quality time together. Perhaps nowadays, there is a sense of urgency to do everything by yourself, to be in control, but I see no harm in relying on others. After childbirth, I was just happy to be looked after and Vishal and I graciously accepted the help. I followed the traditional post-birth Gujarati diet for six months, of gund raab (a sweet soup made with gum crystals), shiro (a sweet dish also known as halwa) dripping in ghee (clarified butter), aubergine curry, spinach curry and millet chapatti – to name just a few delights which helped me gain my strength back and recover fully.

During my pregnancies, I practiced yoga and meditation, chanted mantras and sang and listened to spiritual songs (bhajans), which made me feel balanced and allowed me to provide the early sanskars (habits or impressions) to my children. I went back to work after both maternity leaves with mixed feelings of excitement and worry, as I am sure many new mothers do. Would I be able to cope? Would my son be okay at nursery without me? Although we do not live in an extended family, we continued to have the support of my mother and mother-in-law who would come and stay each week (from Surrey and Birmingham!), helping with the nursery drops and pick-ups so I could be at my desk for 8.30am each day in Canary Wharf. It was perhaps the most challenging time of my career; striving to ensure my work progression was still on track whilst juggling the competing demands of work and deadlines, but also ensuring balance with home life. As any new parent and young family knows, you get through it!

Supporting those in our community is a value established in my family long before I was born. When my maternal grandfather moved to England from Kenya in the late sixties, he was instrumental in helping other families from the Oshwal community (originally from a small village in Jodhpur called Ossiya in Rajasthan, India) who arrived from Nairobi, Kenya to settle in England. My grandparents had decided to move because they wanted a better life for their children, and our family was one of the first Gujarati families who immigrated to South London. They had an open door policy for new arrivals, meaning that as families travelled from the Gujarati Oshwal community in Kenya to London, they were given my grandfather's name as a contact who would be able to assist and many stayed in the family house, sharing meals with them until they could find their own home in the area. Caring for others within our community and keeping close family bonds is a huge part of Gujarati tradition, and this made it a lot easier for those who migrated to England to adjust to a new life. My grandfather was a very disciplined and organised gentleman. He worked at Selfridges in London and took great pride in his appearance – always dressed in a grey suit and white shirt. He was meticulous in everything he did and this is something that he passed down to us, be it life admin or, as friends joke, my somewhat OCD tendencies.

Community work (known as 'sewa' in Gujarati culture) is something that has been central to my parents' and in-laws' from Kenya and remains a big part of our life here in the UK. I was born into a family that highly values the act of sewa which I have fully embraced in my life and which Vishal and I have passed down to our children. As Hindus, we live by Dharmic principles: a way of life with a purpose to do good and make the world a better place.

When I was growing up, bonds between family and the connection to our Gujarati heritage were a constant in my life. In 1974, before I was born, my father along with two friends founded the Oshwal Gujarati School in South London, a Saturday language school for children in the local community that continues to operate to this day. I looked forward to attending every Saturday, and have some fabulous memories of my childhood and youth spent learning with cousins and friends. I went on to be a volunteer teacher at the school once I sat my GCSEs, and loved it! At home we only spoke in Gujarati, which at the time was a bit of a chore, but, with the benefit of hindsight, I am so grateful to my parents for insisting on this. My siblings and I are fluent in reading, writing and speaking Gujarati, which means we can converse well with our grandparents and elders. I value this so much that I have made sure our children continue this tradition and also attend the local Oshwal Gujarati school. Even during the Covid-19 lockdown, when the school was closed and we were not able to see my parents, they held daily Zoom classes with their grandchildren. It was so special for me to witness this intergenerational transfer of knowledge, culture and values.

I guess there was a worry amongst my father and grandfather's generations, those who had travelled from India to Africa and then to England, that moving so far from home might mean our culture and identity would fade away. They were determined to hold on to our traditions and to celebrate our heritage. I am so proud of my Gujarati culture and heritage; it is rich in everything from food and clothing to values, and being born and raised in England means that rather than losing my Gujarati heritage, I have gained another perspective on life. I have the pleasure of understanding more than one culture and feel extremely fortunate to be able to embrace the best of both worlds.

While, we may all have differences, I am certain that we all share the need for one thing in life: self-care. Our lives can feel incredibly fast-paced, and for a long time I admit I probably neglected this. It is easy to do this, to become consumed by daily life. My personal inspiration came a few years ago when my son started learning the tabla - Indian drums. Vishal had also learnt to play the tabla as a child and joined in, enabling his passion to resurface and to do something he enjoyed. They both inspired me to also make time to take up singing again, and I was introduced to one of the most talented singers I know, a performer and teacher – who is now my guru. I love to sing bhajans - spiritual songs - which for me is a form of meditation.

More recently, I have also started to exercise, which I had never really taken the time to do before. I don't do anything incredibly strenuous, but am building up strength and getting fitter slowly, and as a result I find I am sleeping and eating better and focusing more on looking after my body and mind. I am learning to be kinder to myself. I believe everybody needs to make time, even if it is a small amount, to truly relax without feeling guilty about taking a break from ticking things off the endless to-do lists!

Life might be a big rush, but as I try and remind myself and my family, we always have time to slow down, to pause, to breathe and to be kind to ourselves and those around us. Teaching my children to be polite, caring, and respectful of the beliefs of others is something I hope will stick with them for life. I believe my purpose is to connect people and bring people together. Following my parent's footsteps (and my grandparents before them), our home is a hub, a place for family to stop for a cup of chai on their journey home back to the Midlands and friends in our community to meet, and it brings me great happiness to host friends and family and keep our door open to all. While it can be difficult due to the fast-paced lifestyle of today, I firmly believe that we always have or should always *make* time for self-care and to be kind to others.

CHAPTER 17

A Liberated Woman

KALPANA DOSHI

Kalpana Doshi is a professional laughter yoga leader who also works full time in visitor experience at the iconic Victoria and Albert Museum in London. She is a dynamic, resourceful, accomplished woman who strongly believes that getting in touch with our spirituality is essential for survival, and she has previously worked as an educator in human values in a spiritual school. Throughout the most difficult times in her life, including divorce, financial difficulties, and single motherhood, Kalpana shared with me that spirituality gave her the strength to push through, to develop herself, and to continue moving forward. Kalpana is devoted to helping her community and supporting others – she has great ambitions for her laughter yoga workshops and developing peoples' understanding of how important it is to engage in stress-relieving activities when we are faced with the everyday hardships of the modern world.

*

I was born and raised in Mombasa, Kenya. My father was born in Mombasa too and my mother was born in Bhuj, India. My father and grandfather were both barristers and my mother and grandmother were both housewives and home makers. We lived in what we call a joint family. Everyone together. I am one of seven children. I have fond memories of most of my childhood. Our dad used to take us at weekends to the beach or drive-in cinema frequently. Other times we went for long drives to the port or light house where we ate snacks and went for walks. I attended a lovely primary convent school called Star of the Sea. My secondary education was at Coast Girls High followed by a secretarial course at Southons College. At the age of 17, I came to London, England.

The reason I want to share my story is in the hope of inspiring others not to ever give up and feel ashamed of anything that has happened to them.

When I was a child growing up in Kenya, my Gujarati Sunday cultural school was one of the greatest joys in my life. We were a close-knit, caring community where we learnt about our culture, prayers, folk songs, traditional Indian dance and much more. It gave me a wonderful sense of belonging. It was a very strict school and didn't encourage boys and girls to mix together. A group of us were friendly and mixed together. That didn't go down well with the elders who ran the school. In those days, there was no mentoring or any understanding of children's behaviour. One fine sunny afternoon when I was twelve years old, the teachers called me and a few other girls up to the front in the assembly, made us stand in front of the entire school, and without any explanation "let us go". I was very confused and disturbed. I thought I must have done something terribly wrong, something horrible, to be humiliated and suddenly excluded from a group I truly loved – this made me feel like I was worthless. I tucked away this sharp feeling that I was not good enough in the back of my mind and carried it with me throughout my life.

When I arrived home that day after the incident, my father scolded me because he said I must have done something terrible for the school to react in that way. I might have been a handful and maybe even a little bit naughty, but I was very friendly, confident and had no problem mixing with both boys and girls. That school treated everybody like brothers and sisters, and it was frowned upon to mix openly with each other. In our culture, we have a special brother's day just like Mother's Day and Father's Day, and I remember I tied a big flower rakhi (similar to a friendship bracelet) on one boy's hand because I wanted to be close to him and be his friend. We were so innocent, we were so young, and my action was treated as if it were criminal. Over forty years later, I think that the heavy criticism of such an early, innocent interaction with a boy deeply affected my personal self-worth and my later contact with men.

When I was married, my husband didn't treat me the way I deserved to be treated, but I didn't know how much I deserved. I thought I could find safety in having a husband; I thought it was better to be in a difficult marriage than to be alone. My family and I moved from Kenya to England when I was seventeen, I took a job instead of taking my A-Levels, and I was married to my husband in my early twenties. He was a white English man, and although mixed-race marriages are common now, it was very unusual at the time and I was lucky that my family were fine with our relationship. Of course, my family has close ties with our Gujarati heritage; like most Asian and Indian families, we brought our language, culture, food, and festivities with us as we would anywhere in the world. I always have and always will stay closely linked to Gujarati culture – it is my mother tongue and my sense of home.

I was married to my first husband for seven years; it was seven years of some of the most incredible and exhilarating experiences of my life – I have swum in the deepest oceans, skied on the highest mountains, rode a motorbike across London working as a courier just for fun in my early 30s and even experienced scuba diving at Rottnest Island in Australia. All this was possible because of my husband. He encouraged me to be myself, live life to the fullest and accepted me for who I was. My life was extraordinary. We had a chalet in Switzerland, a cottage in Kent, and bought our first flat in Buckingham Gate, SW1 and then later on a flat on Abbey Road, St. John's Wood. It was seven years of an unbelievably amazing life, but it was seven years with painful strings attached – it was time spent constantly waiting up for a man who never came home some nights. I put up with my husband cheating on me constantly; I compromised my own happiness out of fear of being alone. I would stand on our balcony and count cars for hours, sometimes I would reach three-thousand-three-hundred and thirty-three, three-thousand-three-hundred and thirty-four, three-thousand-three-hundred and thirty-five, and repeatedly I would go to the temple at four-thirty in the morning for Mangal Arti and worship and pray that I could just know he was safe. I thought it was better than being by myself.

Such painful relationships always seem nearly impossible to escape from; it's tough to realise that you are strong enough to leave. With my husband, I had to realise that it was him who was causing all the damage to our marriage, not me. It was him who was hurting me by his actions, and I didn't deserve to be treated that way – nobody ever deserves to be cheated on, or left alone at home, not knowing where their partner is, afraid that something terrible has happened to them. With low self-esteem, it can be incredibly hard to realise that you never deserve to be treated badly by a partner. It has been crucially important to me that I raise my daughter, Zara, to never settle for anything less than she deserves, because I didn't have the strength to realise that it was better for me to be by myself than to be in a harmful relationship. When my first marriage broke down, I felt guilty and ashamed about getting a divorce, and I was still terrified of being alone. In a terrible state of isolation and depression and desperation to find safety, I met my daughter's father at a party. We were married within three weeks of meeting.

My family disowned me upon my marriage to my second husband, who was of Afghani origin, born and raised in Lahore as a Pakistani Muslim. For nearly three years, I had no contact with my own family, and I have never felt so alone. To make matters worse, my husband made life unbearable for me and my daughter: he was an alcoholic, he was violent and abusive, and when Zara was three years old, I made the decision that I could not be with him anymore. I told him to leave us. It wasn't just about me anymore, I had my beautiful daughter, the gorgeous light of my life, who I needed to put first and I had to divorce her father so that we could live without fear.

The biggest reality check of my life came when my first marriage broke down. I had never paid a bill or put money towards a mortgage, I had always been taken care of by my husband. When we split up, I remember standing at the bank, sobbing at the counter, taking out all of the cash I had and watching my salary completely disappear as I paid the bills I had to pay. "Here you are, take it," I told the woman behind the desk, "take all my money." I didn't know anything about how adult life worked, I had never needed to understand the value of money. When my second marriage ended, I was stronger. I pulled myself together faster; I had a daughter to take care of, and I had no other choice. All of my efforts went into making sure we survived. Zara was three years old, so I was not working at the time because I was taking care of her, but I decided to become a registered child minder because I wanted her to grow up surrounded by other children. Even now, twenty years later, she is still friends with some of the children who I looked after and we are very close with their families. In the hope that Zara won't make the same mistakes I did, I have made sure she understands budgeting and house bills so that she will be ready to be responsible for herself when the time comes.

Single motherhood is never easy, but Zara is the light of my life and as I raised her, I felt like I was accomplishing something truly amazing. She has always been a great achiever – she finished school with great A levels, grade eight in singing, grade seven in piano and violin, and she sang in two choirs and played in two orchestras. It felt really fulfilling to watch her grow and succeed. Zara can see how hard I have worked to make sure she has everything she needs, and she carries this appreciation with her. She was always a quietly strong girl, and with my support and the support of the communities we became a part of when she was young, she is determined and reaches her goals. As a single mother, life is a balancing act: every person has a wheel of life they want to look at with some sense of equilibrium – finances, family, social life, fun, career goals, and spirituality are all things we may want to fit into our lives but sometimes it can be more difficult than others. We must remember not to criticise ourselves when we feel like something is not perfectly balanced; as long as we are trying our best, that is what is important.

We are fulfilled by being a part of our community and therefore something bigger than ourselves. When Zara was growing up, I thought it was key to teach her strong values of community so that she would never have to feel isolated. I made sure she was a part of different clubs, including Brownies and Girl Guides, so that she could be involved in different activities and experience a sense of belonging. We should all be able to come together and support each other in this world. I would really advise other single mothers to get their children involved in clubs or organisations in the wider community that you feel passionate about, so that you can speak with other people in similar situations and feel that you are supported by a group who understands what you may be going through while raising children.

Working as a teacher in a spiritual school was another key part of my life when Zara was younger. I was an educator in human values, meaning I spent considerable time focusing on self-improvement and what was truly important to me. Zara used to take classes every Saturday morning in the spirituality school where I taught, and together now we try and maintain a healthy balance with everything we need to do in life while holding on to our spirituality and community values. I've raised my daughter to be strong, to be smart, and she knows her own worth and what she is capable of achieving.

When I was still with my second husband, I went to marriage guidance counselling; this was one of the best things to come out of the break-up of our marriage, because I had not realised all of the other issues I carried with me, the guilt and shame and fears I had hidden away which were affecting me. My first divorce had a deep impact on me that I had not confronted, and I was ashamed to talk about it. Now, I have no fear, and I don't feel guilty for doing what I needed to do to survive, and I don't punish myself for any mistakes which are lost in the past.

Speaking about divorce openly has been crucial for helping other people who are in the same type of terrible situation that I was in and do not know how to deal with it – when people see that I'm comfortable talking about my own divorces and problems, they feel comfortable and confident that they will also be fine, that they have the strength to leave a partner or to raise a child by themselves if that's what they need to do. Focusing on yourself and reminding yourself of your own power opens the door to a sense of complete liberty, and to a sense of empowerment which helps you to not accept any maltreatment from boyfriends, husbands, friends, family members, or anyone else. The most important part of life is having a clear vision of how you are serving the wider community. We all deserve to be respected, cared for, and supported by those around us – the only way this can happen is if we also look to support others.

From a young age, I carried with me a deeply ingrained belief that I was a bad girl, and I think a lot of my actions were in response to this self-fulfilling prophecy. Without completing my studies in secondary school, I took a job very quickly without thinking about what I was doing. I didn't look back at further education for a long time: I liked working, and there was a job readily available for me, so I went for it. One of my biggest regrets now is that I never went to university, but I think there's always time to achieve our dreams, no matter what age we are. As an adult and a mother, I did an Access course in psychology, philosophy and English and got the highest number of credits in the class which gained me entrance to University. I really enjoy studying and hope to get my degree in the future. Life hasn't been about putting myself first, it's been about putting the needs of my daughter first, but she's a beautiful and successful twenty-six-year-old woman now, and we aren't just surviving, we are thriving. I finally feel like I am in the comfortable, healthy position I deserve and I can pursue my goals. I have gone from being an obese, depressed, unemployed woman to now being a joyous lady enjoying life to the fullest and serving others. I am also 20 kilos lighter (with the help of bariatric surgery) plus I have a fulltime job that I love. This long journey has been quite a rollercoaster and I have come out of it with my head held high.

Spirituality has helped me through the hardest of times. Seven years ago, I participated in a self-development programme called Landmark, which focuses on finding closure from your past and beginning a life with a clean slate – working on myself in this way has been one of the most rewarding experiences of my life. It has allowed me to grow and move forward without a fear of the past. After completing the initial courses in Landmark, I proceeded to take the Advanced Course followed by Self Expression and Leadership Programme, during which you are expected to demonstrate to the programme leaders that you will be carrying forward and executing a project which will make a difference to society in the future. So, not only do we focus on improving ourselves, we focus on improving the world around us.

My own project for the future focuses on continuing to contribute to community and society by working on large-scale organised sessions of laughter yoga. Last year I participated in 'Diwali in Trafalgar Square' in London and delivered a session in the yoga marquee. Laughter is an incredible therapy because our brains don't know the difference between a fake laugh and a real laugh – once you start laughing in the exercise, real laughter kicks in and you feel rejuvenated. I trained as a laughter yoga leader while taking courses at Landmark, and I am now a qualified laughter leader: helping people by providing them with a refreshing, relaxing meditation and laughter yoga sessions. Offering laughter sessions allows me to help others on their own journey, something I have always wanted to be able to do, and my goal is to turn my skills with laughter yoga into a viable business. Laughter yoga helps relieve stress for anybody – I have provided sessions at schools, private events, community centres, care homes for older people and for corporate team building events. I have even done a session at the

Indian High Commission in England – my aim is to increase peoples' awareness and understanding of the power of laughter and yoga as a form of health improvement. Tapping into our own spiritual awareness can be very difficult to achieve, and in the Western world yoga as a form of healing therapy is still relatively new, but there is always time to grow and change. Considering all of the stresses we encounter in daily modern life; it is essential to our survival that we take our mental health seriously. I hope to become one of the best laughter yoga leaders in the country as I spread my knowledge and share my skills.

Spirituality comes hand-in-hand with supporting other members of our society. Your contribution can be as little as one hour of your time volunteering a week, but it can make a huge difference. For my own part, I love volunteering and have participated a few times in different events. Sometimes helping out at the elders Silver Sunday, sometimes, making sandwiches for homeless people. A few times I assisted in a scheme started by Tony Robbins called 'Basket Brigade', where we deliver a Christmas hamper to families who cannot afford to buy much at Christmas time. Firstly, we spend the day making the baskets together, which is really fun, and then we deliver them with a smile on our faces to the needy in society. I have also volunteered many times on Valentine's Day by delivering roses to older people in care homes. Gestures such as these can make a really big difference in someone's life; the feeling of inclusion is not something we can take for granted. Everybody is equal and deserves the same opportunities. Being part of a wider group and volunteering within the community is fundamental to my Gujarati heritage. We all deserve to feel wanted and respected, and I believe that supporting each other is the only way to move forward and improve our society.

CHAPTER 18

Touring London

KAMU PALAN

Kamu Palan is the Director of Golden Tours, a travel company which she co-founded with her husband Nitin Palan MBE. Employing more than 200 team members in the UK, Golden Tours runs the distinctive blue tourist buses in the heart of London. She is an accountant by profession and a yoga instructor with boundless energy. She travels regularly around the UK and the Indian sub-continent to fulfil philanthropic and teaching duties alongside campaigning for better community relations. She sits on the Board of the company's charitable arm, the Palan Foundation, which supports good causes in the areas of education, health, interfaith and heritage. Kamu's beauty and kindness impressed me and her story is genuinely intriguing. I was captivated by her entrepreneurial spirit and how her ingenuity has led her to succeed in leading a fulfilled life.

*

Trafalgar Square was one of the first places my brother Manu took me when I arrived in London. I remember thinking how beautiful the statues were, surrounded by numerous pigeons. I was liberated when my brother taught me how to get around the city using public transport. Eventually, I acclimatized and embraced the best of British whilst preserving my East African roots. At sixteen, I was smart and as life unfolded in London, I soon learnt that I could accomplish anything with hard work and persistence. Trafalgar Square was to become a special place for me in the future, Diwali in

London would be celebrated there some twenty-eight years later founded by the ambitious dream of my husband and a few friends. It was a vision of sharing the spirit of Diwali with the world, beginning with London. The spirit of love, sharing and celebrating in harmony - I was to be part of this big dream.

I was born in a small village called Mwanza in Tanzania (East Africa) at a time when many people from Gujarat were migrating in search of a better life. My father was from Raval and my mother was from Porbandar in Gujarat, India. The arranged marriage of my father and mother was usual in those days where she was only eleven years old and my father was eighteen. They travelled for thirty days, a perilous journey, together in a ship from India to Tanzania in harsh conditions to settle in a new land. My mother was a child bride and she was thrust into a new culture, language and family. She was a meek fifteen-year-old when confronted with motherhood, cleaning the floor whilst squatting and unaware that she was giving birth to her first child in the kitchen! My mother endured huge adversity in her life, but for her it was the unknown that kept her sane, along with her pragmatism. She was eventually mother to eleven children and suffered the pain of losing two of them in early childhood.

My parents had accumulated some wealth in the early days through the family business. However, regrettably it became apparent that my father was easily led astray and as a result they eventually lost everything. My eight siblings and I lived a very simple and impoverished life and that was our misfortune. There were times when my father wasn't working, and we'd have no food in our little house. The neighbours would come by and ask my mother if she'd finished cooking for the day and she would just pretend that she'd already made pans full of rice and dhal for us to eat. However, the reality was a stark contrast, where my sister and I would pick raw pawpaws off tree branches for lunch. Pawpaws are fruits that have a sweet, custard flavor somewhat similar to banana, mango, and cantaloupe, and are commonly eaten raw. We would splash them with salt and chilli powder and that would be our meal for the day. It was like that for about a year and a half. Despite all this hardship, my mother still emerged strong and resilient.

It was once I'd finished my O-Levels that my brother Manu invited me to London. He was already living there and worked as a car mechanic. He kindly invited me to join him in England in 1973 and suggested that I continue with my studies in London. At that point I'd never been anywhere, being so naïve. However, he had faith in me. He confirmed my travel arrangements and at that time it was difficult to get a direct visa to enter the UK from Tanzania. I was instructed to travel to Dublin via Germany, where he would pick me up at the airport in the Republic of Ireland. It sounded like a simple trip, but for a sixteen-year-old that had never travelled on her own before, it was a daunting experience. I landed in Germany, disembarked and didn't comprehend how I was supposed to get on a connecting flight to Dublin. In the passenger lounge, I sat twiddling my thumbs, expecting someone to guide me to the next flight. I waited and the gate was becoming more and more deserted. It was only thanks to a chance encounter with a handsome American man that sat down at my table and asked where I was going. When I showed him my ticket, he ordered me to run with him to the gate, begging the aircraft staff to let me on, explaining that I didn't speak English. Finally, they allowed me to board but unfortunately it all happened so fast that I didn't have time to thank the kind gentleman.

My luck continued on the plane, where I was seated next to a friendly Irish couple. Despite not understanding their accent, they were so nice to me.

They made sure I ate and gave me a Coca Cola, which I'd never even heard of before. They enquired where I was staying when I arrived in London and seemed shocked that I didn't know what area – in truth, I had no idea how big the city was at the time. They proceeded to help me – at immigration when I was initially refused a visa, and then later at arrivals when I failed to recognize my own brother! It was only when he introduced himself that I realized it was truly him. I broke down crying at the sight of him. The couple gave me their number, written on a piece of paper and told me to contact them if I ever needed anything. I was so grateful, such kind supportive people who ensured that I arrived at my destination safely.

After passing my A-Levels, I went to Kilburn Polytechnic to study accountancy. I absolutely loved it there. The lecturers and tutors were always supportive, and it had a multicultural vibe. My friends were Lebanese, Pakistani, Iranian – we'd all come into the country as youngsters and our thinking was aligned which helped us bond. It was around the same time that I started working at Sainsbury's as a shelf stacker, that I realized the strength of my tenacious character. No job was too difficult for me. I am pragmatic, much like my mother, and I wanted to succeed and have a great life. I didn't want to be a housewife. I wanted to make my own money and be ambitious.

Perhaps this was partly why I declined many marriage proposals – I wanted to be a nurse or an independent spinster! But then at twenty-four, I met my husband, Nitin. He was very keen on me from the moment he saw me and eight months later he asked me to be his wife. I sought my mother's advice and she reassured me that he was an ideal match for me. With a leap of faith and little hesitation, I married Nitin and started a phenomenal adventure with him.

It wasn't long before we embarked on our first venture together. One day, he came to me and said that he wanted to start his own crisp business. He'd heard about a little town in Indonesia that specialised in a particular kind of crisp and he wanted to capitalise on the opportunity. I encouraged him to pursue the idea. Meanwhile, I continued working as an accountant for a company called Mundo Gas, just to make sure that we still had money coming in to pay the bills. It was a beautiful time, just the two of us living in Finchley together, chasing our dreams.

The crisps would arrive in a big lorry and we'd spend evenings and weekends packaging them. We started off by selling in Indian markets and then I thought, why not expand the business to include roasted peanuts too? It's a snack we used to eat a lot back home in Africa so I went about making them myself – boiling, microwaving and adding salt until they reached a good enough standard. I had a full-time job but every night I would make a fresh batch to be packed and sold the following day. I'd manage to squeeze in a few hours' sleep and then I'd wake and go straight to my other job. It was intense but my husband and I were incredibly driven. We didn't want to spend the rest of our lives working for anyone else and we wanted to build something we were proud of – something that we'd done all by ourselves without help from our parents.

The hard work paid off when we secured a deal with the world-famous Harrods store in Knightsbridge, London. By this point I was also making the crisps myself, and so we went to them with a proposition to sell our homemade goods. They tasted them there and then (along with a Coca Cola that I'd brought with me to show how the two things complemented each other) and we were given an order on the spot, with the proviso that we used the prestigious Harrod's packaging instead of our own. We agreed, and so every night after that was spent cooking and packing so they could be delivered first thing. At one point my mother-in-law returned from India and chastised Nitin for working me too hard, but honestly, I was loving it. Working together is so much fun and it was a pleasure to be making such a positive contribution to my husband's family. We were working towards a better life.

I have the same deeply ingrained work ethic to this day. I have a son Mikesh and a daughter Millie and they often say to me: "Mum, if it was me in your shoes, I don't think I'd be able to do it." But I can't ever remember saying oh my God, I'm really tired — not once. I think the more that you tell yourself you're tired, the more you need to take breaks — it's a matter of training your body and your mind so that you can overcome it. I can proudly share that both of my children have demonstrated theses values and never shy away from hard work. My children had enormous faith in me and they encouraged me to pursue a course in yoga. I am indebted to them both for it and would add that yoga is my life and my life is yoga.

This attitude is prevalent in everything Nitin and I have undertaken together. At one time, we were both working in a restaurant called Albasha, located just behind Harrods. But when that place closed down, the restaurant's chef approached Nitin and asked him to take care of the finances for a new version of Albasha that was opening on Kensington High Street in London. Nitin agreed, and before long, I was integrated into the team. I'd go to the restaurant in the evenings and at weekends to work on their accounts, alongside my full-time job. By this point we'd decided to wind up the crisps business, and then Nitin was offered another opportunity, this time with an interior design company called Linea Riva. With so many things going on, it made sense that I stepped into a fuller role at Albasha to help him, and so I resigned from my job and started working full time at the restaurant as an accountant, focusing on all the administration and accounts for both businesses.

Our lives can be characterised like this – seeing an opportunity and grabbing it with both hands. In our minds it's about being brave and having faith in yourself so we are both big risk takers and this made us industrious. I never look back once I've made a decision. At times I'm sure we could have made more money – like with the Harrods deal, for instance, but I have no regrets. I learned from that experience and once it was over, I moved on.

Sure enough, it wasn't long before another opportunity presented itself. It was a hot summer's day and we were both working at the restaurant when a coach broke down outside. Nitin was there immediately offering to help and inviting everyone inside to cool down with a drink. The waiters and I were running around trying to get everyone sorted and meanwhile, Nitin got talking to an Irishman called Ronnie McShane. It turned out that the coach was full of concierge workers who were part of the same sightseeing company. Ronnie was full of praise about the restaurant and after chatting for a while, he asked to come back later that evening to discuss a proposal.

That night, I suppose you could say our lives were changed. Ronnie returned and presented us with an idea that we couldn't resist. He said that we'd done a great job with the restaurant and would we be interested in going into the sightseeing business. We explained that the restaurant wasn't ours – we only owned 30 percent and we had no money of our own – but he persisted. He showed us a brochure for the company he was working for and said that it would likely go bust in a few months' time because it wasn't doing well and they were having staffing issues. His plan was to collaborate with us and we would all go into business together. “I think you guys would make a really good go if it,” he said with confidence.

Back at home, Nitin and I discussed it and he was keen to take the plunge so we decided to do it. We didn’t have any money at the time but we used our savings to put £1000 into the kitty and that was our starting point. Nitin was still busy with all our other projects and so I ended up taking on a lot of the responsibilities at the beginning. And from there, I just figured it out. About a week later we began working on our first brochure, fine tuning what we wanted to say even though I didn’t know anything about Buckingham Palace or other prestigious sites in our iconic London! When the brochure was ready I went back to Ronnie and the team to say we needed help to get it printed but it became clear that the only thing they could offer was their support — they didn’t have any money! This was quite the revelation and so we were flabbergasted but it didn’t deter us. It was risky but we still thought, right, let’s just go for it. As I said, I think if you work hard then God is with you and you will always make it.

We continued like this, using our gut instinct and taking risks in an unknown field. Thankfully, the concierge team really did give us all the support they could — they stopped selling other companies and directed everyone to us. Nevertheless, it wasn't easy. I had a hellish time with guides and staff not turning up. I would have no choice but to step in until we found someone to replace them and I would just stand at the front of the coach and ask the passengers to bear with me. But step by step, it grew, and eventually we decided to concentrate all our efforts on this business. Eventually, we left Albasha and Linea Riva and started Golden Tours and of course, I don't regret a thing. That was in 1984 and we truly started with nothing. I had a basement office with one desk and no money, and I would do everything myself because I couldn't afford a cleaner or an assistant or anything like that. Today, we have 70 vehicles, over 200 staff, and five visitor centres across London as well as a call centre in Ahmadabhad, India. The overwhelming success of the business can be attributed to my son Mikesh. He is now the managing director and with his expertise as a mathematician, he has taken the company to the next level.

With the growing success of Golden Tours we decided to set up a charity and that's when the Golden Tours Foundation was set up. Our aim was to help underprivileged girls in India by providing education. Our belief is that with education you can give a gift to a child for a lifetime. Money comes and goes but with learning, it's theirs to keep forever. This is something I stand by and I am very proud of. The Golden Tours Foundation has now evolved into The Palan Foundation which continues to offer life-changing opportunities for young people to help fulfill their aspirations. It has a broad spectrum of charitable aims nurturing the philosophy of personal, social and economic growth through education. We also assist interfaith communities, such as the Swaminarayan Sanstha in the UK, India and globally.

We've started a pioneering new company called Yantra World. It was my husband's idea, and it's about using IT systems to streamline queuing at attractions. We're very confident that it'll succeed. My passion in business also extends into my personal life in my practice of yoga. I have dedicated a huge amount of time in attending lessons with various teachers and gurus and applied these techniques to further enhance my own practice which was spurred on by my children. It transpired that I had a flair of sharing my learning with others, and now teach yoga. It took me nine months to learn the practice of yoga to teach others.

When my husband and I would travel to India on business every so often we would take a weekend break, driving three hours to Sarangpur, Gujarat. The place where my guru Parmukh Swami Maharaj resided, and it was a place of solace and worship for us. In the evenings I would diligently practice my yoga moves in the privacy of my room with my iPad and books whilst my husband spent time talking to the Sadhus. Pramukh Swami Maharaj was Bhagwan Swaminarayan's fifth spiritual successor. He led by example; his humility, faith in Bhagwan Swaminarayan, and compassion inspired millions of devotees and over a thousand sadhus to maintain moral and spiritual lifestyles. His was the simple life of a celibate, ignoring fame and recognition. His greatness lay in his ability to relate to the common man. He understood the problems people face in their everyday lives and empathised with their pain. Our spiritual life and moral development stem from following such a humble man through these auspicious visits in India. Even though I was born in East Africa, I remain connected to India.

The health benefits of yoga are tremendous and through the integrated system of education for the body, mind and inner spirit, you can achieve simple living and high thinking. I have achieved so much in business and my main focus these days is in helping people and the community through teaching yoga and though my philanthropy. I have a project called Better Women that I want to pursue because my ultimate goal is to make a difference in people's lives. And everyone can do that – you just have to be brave and believe in yourself. That's my strongest message, I think. Never be lazy – even when you're distracted by fun, work hard and you will reap the rewards. I am proof that it works.

CHAPTER 19

Gifts from my Mothers

CHANDNI VORA

It is said that: "A strong woman stands for herself, a stronger woman stands for everyone else." No one epitomises these words more than Chandni Vora, the Chief Operating Officer at Vascroft Contractors Ltd; a female businessperson in a male-dominated business.

Chandni Vora symbolises the strength, perseverance, resilience and business acumen that women from the Gujarati community are known for. The second-generation executive in the family-run company has had an extremely challenging life, but through it all she has kept her determination, positivity and the 'can do' attitude that has made her an inspiration to her family, friends, and peers. Despite the tragedy of losing her mother at the age of ten, Chandni had the strength and independence to build up an impressive 14-year career, working for the likes of Bechtel Inc, BAE Systems, Cable & Wireless, NTL and Majestic Wines, before joining the family firm. This brought new challenges as she joined the male-dominated construction industry, in the company set up by her father and uncle - Vascroft Contractors. Her energy, enthusiasm and vitality are contagious.

*

Prema ('beloved') mum gave me so many beautiful gifts, my life for one and the values that she instilled in me together with the skills that I use to overcome any adversity. She was born in a village in Kutch, Gujarat, and spent her youthful years in South India, in Villupuram, near Chennai, where her family had relocated in pursuit of a better life. Her dark brown plaited hair, round innocent face, bright smile and warm cuddly body will always remain etched in my heart. She wore a saree and bindi which signified the marital status that she embraced. Life for her in the UK once married to my father was a contrast to Villupuram, but she eagerly delivered her duties with diligence and pride. She was the eldest daughter-in-law of a busy household, serving my dad and his four brothers alongside my grandparents. That was a commendable task in my view. I adored my mum's patience, tolerance and intelligence. The wisdom that she imparted will be the greatest gift of her love. I was ten years old when my mum passed away, the day that I had to step up and be the most responsible and mature version of myself.

Life presents you with so many challenges despite your age, and I have learnt to embrace it all. Life also gives you beautiful gifts, and when my dad remarried, he gave us our wonderful, beautiful Jasu ('brainy') mum. She is a stunning woman with big almond eyes, slim body and gorgeous hair. Soon after being married to my dad, she gave us two adorable baby sisters. Life was more settled with our family of six, united in love, respect, acceptance and trust. Embracing a large extended family at the green age of twenty-seven, coupled with two children aged eleven and nine, must've had its challenges for mum. But Jasu mum just acknowledged her duties and seamlessly executed them without any complaints. That was her strength of acceptance and she loves us as her own, caring and supporting us through the various stages of our lives over the last thirty years.

Not only have these two outstanding mothers contributed to my upbringing, values and virtues but my father Shashi has had to play role of mother and father, along with the many inspirational mothers of my childhood friends who have moulded me into who I am today.

I believe my family's powerful, determined attitude towards life has been with us for generations, dating back to my grandfather, who moved to East Africa from Kutch in Gujarat, in the 1950s. Kutch is famous for its *Great Rann of Kutch*, an enormous white salt desert that lies within the boundaries of the Thar desert. The endless white fields of salt are truly a wonder India is blessed with. Kutch is also a place known for its artistic handicrafts, *ari bharat,* sewing mirror discs intricately onto either cotton or silk fabrics along with the tie-dyeing art of *Bandhani Sarees*. The women and mothers of Kutch have remarkable resilience as hard-working women running households alongside farming the land. Such resilience and determination was prevalent when 300 women, including my grandmother, of my ancestral village *Madhapar*, on 8 Dec 1971 were assigned to reconstruct the Bhuj airport air strip for The Indian Airforce during the conflict of that time. They managed to accomplish this in 72 hours, risking their lives. These virtues and skills have been handed down for generations in this region from mother to daughter.

It was from India that my great grandfather decided to leave in pursuit of work - at the time, the East African railways were being built, initially moving to Nairobi, before realising the opportunity was greater in Kampala, Uganda. The entrepreneurial Gujarati spirit was powerful in Uganda, and the Asian population were heavily involved in running the economies of East Africa at the time. Later, I completed a dissertation on Ugandan Asians and their approach to business in Africa. My grandfather married my grandmother in Kampala, and they raised their six children there. Moving across continents, my grandfather found construction work and made a life for his family. Subsequently teaching my father at the age of sixteen how to build a house from its foundations during his school vacations, hence passing this gift to him stating: "No-one can take your knowledge away" – a moto that gave my dad courage to start his construction business in the UK. However, in 1972, Asians living in Uganda became victims of one of history's most blatant displays of cultural prejudice in the African continent. The Ugandan President Idi Amin ordered the expulsion of the country's Asian population, displacing tens of thousands from the place they called home. The British gave us a choice: return to India or come to the UK.

My dad and his brother had humble beginnings when they arrived in England from Uganda. They started working in manual labor jobs in construction. Accommodation was supplied by friends of the community where they lodged, leaving them with little money to save. Strong willpower and grit were a necessity because there was nothing else; they arrived with very little, and they had to believe in themselves. 'Cannot' was not a word in dad's dictionary; in life, we must find our willingness to maintain strength, even when things are difficult. By the time I was born, three years after my dad moved to England from Uganda, he had a bought a house for my grandmother and his brothers to live in Wembley, whilst employed as a laborer working on building sites at the Barbican Towers in London. In 1974 my father registered his company as SK Vekaria Builders Ltd, a carpentry business and then two years later he enrolled his younger brother Arjan to join soon after completing his HND in Quantity surveying. Shashi (my dad) and Arjan went into partnership to start Vascroft Contractors Ltd in 1977 and that is how the name Vascroft, V- Vekaria, A- Arjan and S – Shashi was created. My dad wanted his brother's name before his own name as he expressed that: "Family has to succeed before I succeed." This attitude is so important to me too. Put others before you. We are nothing without our community and kin. Vascroft has been running successfully for the past 43 years despite bearing the sad loss of uncle Arjan in 2013.

Racism was prevalent in England in the 70s when my dad set up and being taken seriously as Indian businessmen was challenging. There was an awful racist sentiment that Ugandan Asians were coming over and stealing jobs. And this is the reason why my dad and his brothers decided to add 'croft' to the business name, a commonly heard place name-ending used in the UK, which refers to farmland or buildings, to make their business sound more serious and trustworthy. They wanted people to be aware that they were a business who could reliably deliver projects with trust and integrity. In the 80s Vascroft got a break in the hotel market due to a Punjabi developer who had faith in them. Then the clients started to roll in, and the company worked on more hotels before attracting contracts in the high-end residential market.

My dad does not perceive any limits – “If there are 25 hours in a 24-hour day, make it 26,” he proudly tells me. No one else will make the time except you. If ever I am having a hard day and need some motivation, I remind myself of my dad’s strength and resilience. I am indebted to my dad for supporting my brother and I after my mother died, we were both so young: I believe that her death, when I was only ten years old, has made me feel like I have the strength for anything the world throws at me.

When my dad told us that our mother had passed away, I just looked at him in shock. Though my brother broke down, I didn’t cry. At such a young age, I decided I needed to be the one to hold it together; I wanted to be strong for my brother. I think that losing our mum made us both feel that self-reliance was incredibly important. Letting go of my emotions has always been really hard for me, because I think of everything my mother went through, of how hard she worked for us and the extended family, and I try not to have any self-pity and instead focus on moving forward, because I believe there is always someone who has more difficult circumstances than I have had. Faith and gratitude can be found even in our darkest moments.

Before her death, my mother was ill for a long time. When I was nine, she had serious problems with inflammation in her legs, resulting from a thrombosis clot. I still remember her going to hospital in the middle of the night, and finding out the next day that she was in a coma. I kept thinking, it's fine, it's all going to be fine. But after two weeks passed, the doctors told my dad they didn't think my mother was going to come out of her coma - they told him it was time to bring his children in to visit her and say goodbye. Before we entered the intensive care unit, my dad paused, looked at both of us, and warned us: "When you see mum, just know she doesn't look the same. Don't be afraid, she can hear you, so you should talk to her, and she knows what you're talking about." It was so shocking to see her look so fragile in the hospital bed. She had lost so much weight, and she had tubes all over her. My brother was very emotional, and my father had to keep reassuring us that we needed to keep chatting to her.

The very next morning after our visit to the hospital, my mum woke up. But she woke up without being able to move her limbs or even speak - she tried to say our names, but it was hard to understand her. As my mother began her rehabilitation, my brother and I would visit her every day after school. We started taking her Sanskrit and Gujarati books to read - she was an incredibly clever lady who had been a Sanskrit scholar and mathematician. When she was able to talk and walk again, she came home, and I would help her in the house a lot. Self-sufficiency became important to me when I was so young out of necessity: I needed to be there to help my mother. I used to help my mother put on her beautiful south Indian silk saris for family events whilst she was recovering. My mother had been a phenomenal cook before her illness - she had taught me to make a huge variety of Gujarati meals, and I remember people used to come to her to learn how to make dosa (a South Indian pancake). When she moved back into the house and was rehabilitating, it was me showing her how to cook now instead - a complete role reversal. We'd cook together, maybe an aloo (potato) curry, and I helped to teach her culinary skills along with my grandma.

My mother's memory was coming back at warp speed and the doctors advised her to go home, back to her roots in Kutch, Gujarat and Villupurum, Tamil Nadu where she grew up, to help her strength grow and her memory return. She'd learned to write again, and I still have the letters she sent me from India while she was there with family. Unfortunately, while she was still in India, she ended up in the hospital again with a lot of complications, and she died on 28th February 1987.

I am constantly inspired by my dad's strength in the face of all the hardship he has experienced. He, along with both my mothers' teachings built my foundations. I share his bold, determined attitude; he always reminds me I could do anything if I put in the effort. If there are roadblocks, we want to find our way to overcome them as quickly as possible. When I was fifteen and halfway through my GCSEs, my secondary school shut down - most schools wanted me to sit back a year. But I wanted to get to university as soon as possible, finish my studies, and get a job - slowing down on this path was not an option - 'cannot' was not an option - so I took it upon myself to find a new school that would take me without delay.

When I was studying my A-Levels a year later, I decided I wanted to be as successful on my own as my father had been. I opted for a career in finance by graduating from CASS. My professional experience thus far has allowed me to make connections and build friendships with people that have provided life-changing advice and inner progression.

I strongly believe that practical experience is just as important as academic achievement, if not more. When I was fourteen and received my National Insurance Number, I started doing 6am paper rounds. My brother and I divided the days of the paper round, and whenever we got paid we split our wages and would do something nice together, like see a film. At sixteeen, I started working at McDonalds at the weekends, allowing me to build my business awareness. Working for such a big company meant I was learning about quality management - McDonalds' brand and appearance is key, and I wanted to understand how they operated their quality assurance. During my university years I worked weekends at Boots plc appreciating the importance of teamwork and commitment. Whenever you're working, you always have the option to go in, take your wages, and go home - but you also have the option to pay close attention to how the business functions, and learn from it. This hands-on experience at an early age was truly invaluable and brought out my entrepreneurial spirit.

Upon graduating, Bechtel Engineering hired me as the group financial management accountant, and placed me in the Europe, Africa, and Middle East team. Suddenly, I was reporting on construction projects around the globe, reporting to HQ in San Francisco. As an Asian woman, it felt incredible to be chosen - to have that stamp of approval, that assurance that the company valued me. Working for a global company was exactly what I had been working so hard for, since I was that fifteen-year-old girl who had battled her way into a new school without having to stay back a year. I was always focused on a clear goal: work hard and make it on my own. My impatience for things to get done as quickly and efficiently as possible was clear: When I first joined, the company ethos was very blasé, and the branches would submit their reports as and when. But I wanted the information to be streamlined, seeking efficiency, and so I implemented a strategy, revealing that San Francisco had shortened their deadlines to submit their reports. I was in pursuit of excellence and determined to be ahead of other global teams. Shocked at the branch improvement, my manager asked me: "How did you get them to work faster? The guy before you couldn't convince them." I told them there are always ways to empower people to take ownership and deliver results efficiently if shown the right tools.

I am driven by wanting to be my best self. However, I've been learning more recently that everything is best within moderation, and that my urge to be constantly moving and busy can be both a positive and negative trait. Over the fourteen years working for different global organisations, and now, in my role at Vascroft, my efficiency has helped me drive systems and processes. I'm always learning how to take a step back and think about other peoples' perspectives. If I don't see results straight away, or someone does something a different way than how I would usually do it, I have learned to become more patient, that not everybody moves at the same quick pace as me. In my opinion emotional intelligence is paramount. Our differences are what creates the fabric of society.

Patience at home, as well as at work, is something I have also been working on more in recent years. We can always grow and improve as people, regardless of age. While I want to crazily pack a million things into the day and say, right, we're going here, you're doing this, we have to get this done, my husband of twenty one years is the calm in my storm and brings a perspective to my way of being. With our daughters, we both believe it's important for them to be busy and sociable so they can learn from people, but we also recognise how important it is to have quiet time for reflection. I want to inspire my girls to understand that every minute of the day is important - this includes moments of self-reflection, of down time, and focus on strengthening our mind muscles of non-judgmental acceptance.

Married at the tender age of 23 as many from our Shree Kutchi Leva Patel community were during those days, I was able to hold onto the teachings of my mother's experience of extended families of tolerance and kindness, allowing me to build a unique relationship with my mother-in-law. Another exceptional compassionate human being to have influenced my way of being. She too was the eldest sibling of five in her family and was not as fortunate to have a formal tertiary education and was married at the youthful age of 18. Her calm tendency of executing her duties are admirable and she continues to share her great Kenyan culinary skills with me. A few months after we were married, my husband and I were entrusted as guardians of his siblings, a seventeen-year-old sister and twenty-three-year-old brother. This didn't faze me at the time as I had seen how my own mother had taken the duties to look after and provide for my dad's siblings. The ethos of helping them start a new life in the UK migrating from Kenya was the norm. To this day I still have good respectful relationships with my mother-in-law and extended family. Which always came down to a simple fact - treat people the way you want to be treated – be kind and non-judgmental. Gifts bestowed upon me from the past clearly helped me through this married chapter of life.

My passion for Indian classical Kathak dance along with long-distance cycling has played a huge part in growing my patience and helping me feel calmer allowing me to be free in my thoughts as a form of meditation. I'm living with diabetes, alongside many members of my family, and so keeping fit is paramount in improving my health. My mum died at the young age of thirty-six, so I was worried about making sure I lived past that age; fear of leaving my girls behind pushed me to start cycling and get into shape. The virtues of *sewa* - selfless service and giving back to society - have been a generational gift from my parents and grandparents. With that in mind, I have an annual motivational goal to raise funds for various charities. I have participated in the spectacular 100-mile challenge RideLondon in 2015 and 2019 and raised money for the Nepal earthquake and the British Heart foundation. I subsequently inspired my younger sisters to take part in our 2016 London to Paris challenge of a gruelling 286 miles on behalf of Diabetes UK. I also completed the 26-mile Shine night walk for Cancer Research UK in six hours and twenty-seven minutes and this was only possible with the right mindset. We all have different ways to alleviate stress. The gift of endurance and perseverance passed down to me has also allowed me to complete yearly sporting challenges.

Fulfilment can mean different things for different people: perhaps someone else's path might be totally different from mine, but that doesn't mean it's not right. Each of us has a different path to pave. I have carved my own path in my unique way as this is what I desired, and by continually learning, I found my areas of improvement. My husband has been a great pillar of support for everything that I do - he understands where my professional life is and helps me to move forward on my career path, which is great modelling for my daughters. Now, as a professional businesswoman, wife, and mother, I hope to leave a legacy which inspires my daughters to never see any boundaries on what they can achieve. I aim to ensure our roots in Gujarat and our affiliation to India are bestowed upon our girls. That will be my gift to my daughters, and I can only wish for them to pass these values and virtues on to their children.

Our mindset is often the deciding factor in whether we strive towards success; anything is possible, and we can use strength and grit to reach our goals. A positive mindset transforms everything; a journey might take a while, maybe longer than you expected, but remember: every day is a learning experience that sets you up for tomorrow. Adversity should be embraced with new opportunities which can transform into positivity. Stand tall like a tree with deep roots, stay grounded, keep growing and know when to let go. So, thank you to all my mothers that have impacted my life and given me so many precious gifts.

CHAPTER 20

Global Woman

KRISHNA PUJARA

I had just finished speaking on a panel at the annual Global Woman conference hosted by the pioneering Mirela Sula when I met Krishna, who kindly introduced herself as the Chief Executive of Enfield Saheli. It's a great organisation that aims to enable women to participate fully in the social, cultural and civic life, empowering women. In addition to this,

Krishna has worked within and helped to develop and lead a number of statutory and voluntary sector organisations in the UK, with a special professional interest in supporting health and social care groups. She also has a passion for arts and culture.

I was attracted to her drive to support women and I instantly felt that we would meet again on several occasions, since we resonated in different areas of our professional lives. Her track record of success within community and statutory organisations is truly impressive in promoting the concerns of women regarding domestic abuse, forced marriages, trafficking and Female Genital Mutilation (FGM) in the UK and globally, speaking volumes about her dedication and commitment to communities.

Through her work, Krishna has become an active ambassador and voice of communities: currently she holds executive posts and is the chairperson of the following organisations – ALL (All Ladies League) UK; Women's Wing, Lohana Mahaparishad UK; Domestic Abuse Operational Forum for Violence Against Women & Girls (Enfield); Public Relations, National Congress of Gujarati Organisations UK, Secretary General, The India League & Sardar Patel Memorial Society UK.

Her energy and vision for the community amazes me and her role as president of UK-India Business Council of WICCI (Women's Indian Chamber of Commerce & Industry) is testament to her power of connectivity. In recognition of all of her work and services to the community, she has received awards from various different bodies over the years. Through Krishna's collective approach, her mentorship and friendship has encouraged me to speak at the High Commission of India in London and at the Women Economic Forum in India. Her energy is contagious and her ability to enrol women to be collaborative and inclusive is her strength. Krishna shared her story with compassion and integrity, for which I am immensely grateful.

*

Driving around in my red convertible Mercedes in London in the early eighties made a lot of heads turn. I was in my twenties and thriving in a high-flying career working as a million-dollar financial consultant in the insurance industry. I was even flown out to Los Angeles for a week to meet the top guys in the financial market, where I was interviewed by Michael Douglas on his TV show together with an upcoming star, sixteen-year-old American actress and model - Brooke Shields. "Here we have an Indian woman who has never been to India!" he said, and curiously asked me questions which allowed me to explain that I was British Indian, and that my parents had been born in Africa. We talked about how I had become a member of the financial services association Million Dollar Round Table. When the interview was finished, I spent a whole week in Los Angeles and had trips arranged to visit Hollywood and Beverly Hills - I loved every second of it.

I think a lot of people were envious of my success at such a young age, but everything I earned, I earned myself: I started working incredibly hard at age fourteen when I moved to England from Tanzania with my brother and sister. As a third-generation Indian woman, my parents' families both originated from Gujarat, and my great grandparents had migrated to East Africa - my mum had grown up in Uganda, and my dad in Tanzania.

My siblings and I were raised in my birthplace - Mwanza, Tanzania, where we were protected with a happy, luxurious life - we were really shocked by the immediate culture change when we arrived in England without our parents. London felt so gloomy and cold and there was significantly less socialising than we were used to. It was a difficult struggle for a long time. We stayed with our aunt, renting out rooms in houses because it was so expensive to rent a whole property. We missed home a lot, and all decided to take up part-time jobs to save enough money for plane flights back for the holidays. When I did travel back to Tanzania, though, I felt so confused - I realised after a few weeks that even though I missed my family and familiar comforts, I wanted to continue studying back in England, and that it was better to stay in London.

So I kept on working: I'd study all day, then work at the supermarket as a cashier in the evening. When I finished my A-levels, I decided I didn't want to study anymore because I wanted to earn money straight away. I worked in a post office from nine to five, and then in the evenings I would work in the supermarket for three more hours. Time off wasn't important to me, even at the weekends I'd do a shift just to make as much money as I could. When I was in my early twenties, I decided to increase the pace, and began working in the financial company where I eventually became a Million Dollar Round Table member and consultant.

Then, at the height of my career, I decided to get married, and everything changed. I met my husband, who is also Gujarati, in Kenya when I was travelling back to meet family. After our meeting, we continued to be in touch, because he was so interested in me. I loved all the attention he gave me; I could see how much he loved me, and I decided to marry him. But it came at a cost: he lived in Kenya, and he wanted me to move there with him. My brothers were against me getting married because they didn't think it was a good idea for me to return to live in Africa. But I didn't listen. With love in my heart, I gave up everything I had worked for and moved to Kenya.

Suddenly, I was locked in all the time. In Kenya, I lived with my husband and his extended family, and security issues meant we almost never went outside. I couldn't even go for a walk by myself. If I wanted to go shopping, the tradesmen would come and sell their merchandise to us at home. I wasn't making money anymore, so if I wanted to spend anything, I had to ask for money, meaning I had little to no independence. One day, I just got so fed up and decided to go for a walk, but when I came back after about half an hour, everyone at home was stunned. "Where have you been?" they all asked me, and when I said I just went for a walk, they told me they had got so many calls from people saying they'd seen me walking about. We had everything at home, but I just could not enjoy myself, it was repressive. At around the same time, I had my daughter Chandni, and I realised this restrictive life in Kenya was not for me.

If you're not happy, do something about it. Nobody deserves to suffer. As a new mother, it was so hard to make the choice to leave, but the environment in Kenya was completely different to what I was used to in England, and despite all efforts, It was very difficult to adjust to the demands. Now on reflection, I realised that my in-laws also had expectations which I couldn't fulfil, so the situation was just incredibly difficult for everyone involved. The incompatibility in our values and family perspectives was complicated, and I was left feeling ashamed. Further contemplation has made me realise that we just weren't a good fit, and there is no one to blame for this. Thinking about leaving frightened me because I knew it would upset my family. I knew they had a reputation to uphold in Kenya which would be disturbed by my leaving. I also feared returning because I had got married without my brothers' families' consent, but in the end, it didn't matter - I had to leave and do what was best for me and my daughter.

When I returned to London, it dawned upon me that the financial world had moved forward incredibly quickly during the five years I'd been away. People who had been working for me were now doing really well and had a greater understanding of technology than I did. I'd fallen behind, but that didn't stunt my ambition - I had no choice, I knew I had to start afresh and build my self-esteem and confidence, so, while raising my daughter, I had to develop my skills to get back in action and therefore decided to go for further studies which I had given up earlier. I got my degree in business studies, my master's in business, and eventually my PhD. This was an enormous achievement for me.

In life there's always ample opportunity to learn and whilst I was studying, it became apparent that there was a challenge for students who were balancing their studies and caring for elderly relatives with physical disabilities, with no respite care. A group of us decided to do something about it, and over the next four years, helped campaign for carers support in Brent. When carers' support started to be much better for students, we began to tackle the problems for young school students who were looking after parents with disabilities. Our campaign for young carers was so successful that HRH Princess Anne decided to create the Princess Royal Trust for Carers, which now has over a hundred Carer Centres in England.

My passion for social issues increasingly intrigued me particularly when I was studying part-time for my master's degree and working part-time with the Carers Centre, which led me to uncover issues about domestic abuse, which nobody was really talking about at the time. Refuges for women who were experiencing domestic abuse were few and far between, so not many women could be accommodated.

To further my career, I intended to embark upon more influential work in London in the technology industry. But when I completed my education, my daughter had just turned eleven years old, and I wanted to be there for her. I thought hard about this decision, and I realised that having a high-profile job and commuting in and out of London would take time away from me and my daughter, and I wanted the time to balance work and her future.

Sacrificing a high-profile career was worth it for me, because it meant I was always around after school and able to support my daughter when she needed me. Supporting women with charity work became more important to me than a corporate position. I wanted to pursue work which helped other women - I realised that my priority was to demonstrate strong values to my daughter. While I was working for the Refugee Council, I was invited to join Women's Aid as a volunteer on their Executive Council to help in developing the Women's Aid Refuge: they needed my expertise on how to help women rebuild their lives in a culturally sensitive space. Within weeks, I was appointed President Elect to support and develop the strategic Plan for the organisation. I found out about the women's organisation Saheli, and I decided this was the organisation I wanted to expand and make bigger and better. I'm now the CEO of Saheli, and it has really grown since I became a part of it.

To give my daughter the best life, it was also really important that I maintained a good relationship with my husband. I wanted to make sure that my daughter would have a relationship with her father. Families who are fighting all the time make things so difficult for their children, and I wanted my daughter to feel stable. We've managed to keep a strong connection, and, now that we have recognised that we are better as friends than as husband and wife, we are able to support each other and share our difficulties with each other.

My husband's family are still always very respectful and happy to see me - we have a good link, and I have always prioritised my daughter's ability to travel and visit her relatives in Africa. But it's important that I'm open about the difficulties I faced with my mother-in-law, especially because it's not uncommon for such difficulties to arise with daughter-in-law's entering a new family. When I was leaving Kenya, my mother-in-law would say she didn't think I would be able to survive by myself. Things were a lot more challenging for me, because she made me doubt my own abilities, and it took me some time to recover from the gender inequalities I endured in Kenya.

Someone putting you down over a long period of time, even when it isn't intentional, is incredibly harmful and can only be tolerated to a certain extent. I have moved on from my past because I believe you cannot move on without forgiveness. Nothing is one-sided, and I think perhaps there was more expectation from me, something vastly different from the daughter-in-law of her only son, and our personalities were not well matched. As time passed, I have met my mother-in-law in India while she was visiting relatives. I felt I had enough strength within myself to meet with her and just have a normal, social conversation without any negative topics coming up. Everything that had happened between us was so far in the past, and I was at a point in my life when I felt comfortable with myself and secure in the choices I had made to support my daughter and live an independent life in England.

Leaving a situation which is making you suffer is never easy - in particular for new mums fleeing a home and starting afresh. As the CEO of Saheli and also the chairperson for domestic abuse in the operational forum for Enfield Council, I am in the position to make a difference for these women. After much anguish in my own journey, and struggling to make it with a young daughter, I am driven to ensure women have access to support systems which could make a huge difference to their lives. I am inspired by the knowledge that I can connect immediately with anybody that I am supporting.

Saheli means friend, and although the charity was set up by Asian women, we have an open-door policy and we try to help everyone. We provide a wide range of services, including advice, temporary refuge, therapy and mental health support, securing accommodation, and aftercare. Women from Asian backgrounds often face different problems than perhaps are expected, including language barriers and extended family issues. With my work as the lead for domestic abuse in Enfield Council, I hope to increase representation for all women, elderly women, and women with disabilities, because abuse can affect absolutely anyone, and everyone's needs should be supported.

Refuge spaces are close-knit, and a lot of women have to share kitchens and survive in a tiny room with their children. The lockdown that was enforced by the British government due to containing the spread of the coronavirus in 2020 hugely impacted some women suffering from domestic violence and abuse. Many stories can be told about this challenging and tragic time. Our services also look at other methods to engage with women and men, encouraging women not to leave their homes. By supporting the mild to moderate symptoms of marriage difficulties earlier, it enables us to implement interventions to ensure that couples can live together, and this really helps some marriages. This helps dispel the myth that if you go to support services, you'll be encouraged to leave, subsequently losing your family and ending the marriage. That's simply not our ethos.

Saheli is a team effort: we all work together to achieve our goals. Our work is hard, and can be mentally exhausting, so it's key that we all follow up with each other and make sure we are being supported. When we see we are making a difference in the community, that is very rewarding. Allowing everyone to show what they can do is a crucial part of my working style. The only way I can fit in all the different chairing positions and charity work I do is by delegating work to the supportive team that I have available. You can't do everything on your own - getting help from others is key to achieving success.

My voluntary work with other organisations has helped me to get a sense of self satisfaction, of giving something back to the community.

I joined Brent Indian Association on their Executive Committee and have served in various roles from Executive Committee member Secretary General from 1997-2011.

Being inspired by Sardar Patel's life, I was delighted when I was asked to join Sardar Patel Memorial Society in 2009 as the Secretary General. I continue to provide my services to society to propagate the values of Sardar Patel in the Spirit of Unity.

In 2011, I was invited to join the Executive Committee of National Congress of Gujarati Organisations (NCGO)UK. As a Gujarati, I was delighted to be asked and accepted. NCGO UK is an umbrella organisation for Gujarati Organisations in UK and campaigns for the needs of Gujaratis in the UK. Since then I have been giving my time voluntarily and have served in various roles as Secretary General, Treasurer and at present the Public Relations Officer.

Through my passion to do something for the community, I joined Lions Club in 2007 and have been an active member of London Central Host Lions Club. My efforts have been recognised with the Melvin Jones Fellowship Award for Humanitarian and Charitable work in the community.

I am also part of The India League which was established in 1916, a body which represents the views of British Indians.

We all are aware of the difficulties women face working in a male dominated world. We know that women are better at dealing with crisis and can juggle work with domestic duties. However, the main challenge I have faced is, your work is appreciated – but you will never be good enough to take on the role of the chairman, especially within these male dominated organisations. Over the years, I have made a decision to continue to provide services to make a difference to the community and the positions don't really matter at the end of the day, it is your inner soul that is satisfied with the little difference you have made to society. However, through the Women Organisations I lead, we ensure that we continue to campaign for gender parity.

There are some women who believe that to be successful, they have to crush others. Personally, I believe there is so much space for female success and for women in business and charity to expand their work, we do not need to waste time feeling threatened. I do not believe in competition. You will always get back whatever you give. As a community leader and a president for the UK India Business Council of Women's India Chamber of Commerce and Industry, one of my key focuses is to make sure we reach all women across different industries and foster connections between these women. We want the world to know the stories of these incredible businesswomen and all the hard work they do, and we want them to be able to reach out and connect with each other.

Due to the Pandemic and both lock downs, things are going to get busier, people will suffer more from a range of things that are secondary to Covid-19 and because of this a lot of work needs to be done that we had never planned for or thought about. We will need to reach out to our vulnerable women members going through loneliness and Isolation. We will have to ensure that they are safe and well. Sadly, domestic abuse cases will increase and we will have more demands in our advocacy for mental health services.

The few months of lockdown in 2020 always remind me how important self-care can be. I have regularly meditated, and my outdoor time when I take my dog Leo for a walk is a necessity for me because it gives me some breathing space. I have also realised how important family is to me, and I have had the opportunity to share time with my daughter and enjoy more home-cooked meals together. Often, I do not have a typical nine to five schedule, as I can be so busy with different charities and organisations.

"Our talent we get from our father, but our souls from our mother," said the Russian playwright Anton Chekhov. My journey of life has been amazing, I plunged into new projects without any hesitation. All these endeavours have resulted in interesting interactions and positive experiences. I consider all these initiatives and decisions to launch new ideas, as and when required, as an act of art! A wise person once said: "Knowing when to walk away is wisdom. Being able to is courage. Doing it with your head held high is dignity."

And finally, receiving the one-to-one feedback and seeing the outcomes of cases, knowing I have made a real difference in someone's life, that is the best reward I could ever have. All I want is to make a positive difference for people, and I find that through helping others, I am always becoming a better, more understanding individual.

I believe the following statement: "Strong women aren't simply born. They are made by the storms they walk through."

CHAPTER 21

Panoramic Woman

DR TRISHA RADIA

Dr Radia qualified as a doctor from King's College, London University, in 2002, and now is an acute paediatrician at King's College Hospital working in general paediatrics and high dependency care. She has also attained her Master's in Advanced Paediatrics from University College London. At King's, Dr Radia is the simulation lead for Child Health and developed the award winning

KICCS simulation team there. Away from her clinical role, Dr Radia is a Training Programme Director for the London School of Paediatrics, part of Health Education England, for which she leads on simulation training for postgraduate paediatric trainees and Return to Practice. She runs the well-received Paediatric Return to Acute Clinical Practice (PRACP) Course, which utilises high fidelity simulation coupled with relevant lectures and holistic support, to facilitate the return to clinical practice of any trainee who has had a break in training. Dr Radia has written articles on paediatrics and medical education and has contributed to the upcoming edition of the Oxford Handbook of Acute Paediatrics. Away from medicine, Dr Radia is a mother to two young and very active boys.

Throughout her interview, it was heartening to hear how Trisha has accomplished a tremendous amount in her career and family life. She lives her life with a clear purpose and vision in helping others.

*

As a paediatric doctor my job is not just to provide medical care for children, it is to support the families of these children throughout the entire treatment. As a parent, you have hopes and dreams for your child, and to see a parent go through the loss of a child, or to realise that their hopes and dreams might not be fulfilled because the child has a disability or medical problem, is hard to accept. I found that my role with time and age is to support those families, to ensure they are getting the right care and the right service, because my role might not always be to make a child better, sometimes it's not possible to make them better, but I can always be the listening ear for that parent. Paediatrics is a unique field of medicine because it isn't about looking after just kids, as a child comes with a family unit, and I need to support that family unit.

I have cried every time one of my patients has died. I've cried with our junior doctors and senior nurses; I've sat there and sobbed and hugged the parents of children I've cared for. I'm okay with showing my emotions, because I think it's crucial to deal with death with compassion and empathy. Perhaps people sometimes have this image of doctors as incredibly strong because they deal with death and sickness all the time, but each of my patients who have died have left a scar on my heart. I always teach my junior doctors that it's okay to feel upset. Crying does not make us weak; letting our feelings out helps us to move forward.

Wanting to help people has always been a core value to me - my dad's nature is to help people, he has the compassion of a medic, and I grew up seeing that in him and I inherited this desire to help people from him. As a young girl, I wanted to study medicine, but I didn't think that I could do it, and I think this is partly because my parents were the first generation of my family here in the UK, and we didn't know or believe that was feasible. They were of the generation who just hoped they would be able to get a job - having individual aspirations wasn't as important as making sure you were stable. Growing up I didn't think that I was smart enough to become a medic and I worked exceptionally hard in school and achieved great results. This boosted my confidence and at sixteen years old, I knew nothing could stop me from going into medicine.

Sometimes it can be hard to see yourself for your own talents, because you see people who are smarter than you and can get discouraged. But it doesn't matter what anyone else is doing, as long as you're working hard and have a strong sense of determination. My parents weren't really pushing me to do medicine, which is an important thing to note as I think often, especially as I am from an Indian background, people assume that my parents must have wanted me to do medicine, but there are no medics in my family. I pushed myself to do medicine because it was what I wanted to do.

I fell in love with paediatrics in my fourth year of medical school. When I first started, I thought that I would become a general practitioner (GP) because I didn't really believe I would be able to become a consultant paediatrician. But after I did paediatric medicine during my course, I felt I had found my passion and was determined to become a paediatric doctor. With concern for the hours I was working, I was encouraged by my family to become a general practitioner instead, thinking about my wellbeing. Paediatrics is a big commitment, and it requires extra years of training to specialise after your foundation training with years of overnight resident on calls. But I could not be deterred, because paediatrics is what I enjoyed the most. I like the variety in the field – we care for babies and children all the way up to eighteen-year-olds, meaning we encounter a whole range of different problems. What I love about paediatrics is that every day can be different, and I can do absolutely anything, I'm dealing with kidneys, lungs, and hearts. My specific training is in paediatric high dependency, and I am skilled in stabilising unwell children - I have trained in interventions to stabilise them and then look after them. With children, you can often see a turnaround really quickly, and that is so satisfying because normally, I get to see children start to get better. I like paying close attention to things and seeing a child improve. Paediatrics is a very sociable specialty in the hospital - it's very team-driven, with very little hierarchy, and the nurses and doctors work closely together.

As a paediatric consultant, I'm often on call which means I will sometimes work until very late at night and then I'm available at home for telephone calls to attend the hospital if needed. In Indian culture, it's not traditional for a woman to be on site at her workplace until past midnight, but this is what my job needs from me. Nothing would stop me from doing the work that I love. I've been challenged multiple times about my late working hours, because, of course, these hours mean that I am not home every night to make dinner or look after my family every evening. For my children, it's easy to understand what 'on call' means, and they know that on the nights when I'm on call they will have to wait to see me in the morning. My husband is very supportive, and he can cook if I am working. Together, we juggle everything, and we make it work as a family. The only thing that is important to me is that my partner and I feel comfortable in our own decisions.

I don't believe that I should have to ignore or hide my Indian heritage because of my job, and I don't think that doing a job with non-traditional hours makes me any less close to my Indian culture. I know I can be a consultant paediatrician and integrate with my Indian culture as well - I shouldn't have to make a choice of one or the other.

When I was growing up, I was very much an Indian girl, and I never wanted to hide it. I think that Gujarati culture means being open, accepting, humble and hard-working, and I embrace these qualities in everything I do, including in my workplace. I am very much British Asian - my parents are both Gujarati, but my dad is from Uganda and he fled during the expulsion period, and my mum is from Tanzania. They met and got married here, and I was brought up in Harrow, which is a very Indian populated area, so for my early life I was very much surrounded by Indian culture. We had a big family living near us and that's really important to me, and I am still very close to my cousins and extended family. My environment changed a lot, however, when we moved to Surrey and I started attending a Catholic secondary school where I was the first non-Catholic, and one of the only brown people in the school. I experienced a certain level of discrimination or microaggressions and lack of understanding from people about where I was from, and this meant that from a young age I was defending my heritage and refusing to let go of it. Just because I wasn't surrounded by my culture, that didn't mean I needed to change who I was.

I have evolved in my various roles both personally and professionally. The endless opportunities in my profession have introduced me to medical education. Over the past six years, I've been training in simulation programmes for medicine, and I am now a training programme director and look after simulation programmes for London. We deliver simulated medical scenarios for our trainees, and I specifically look after mainly those coming back to clinical training after being away from the workplace.

Some of my work as a Training Programme Director is learning from incidents in hospital. Medicine is a very reflective specialty, although rare for things to go wrong, when they do, we study it and explore why, we carry out a root cause analysis as to what went wrong and appropriately implement changes. There are many cases that have been reported in the press about deaths and errors within the hospitals, but the key is how to implement learning as a wider team and group. On reviewing cases like this, you will find, it is never down to one person, it is typically system issues, human factors, a breakdown in communication and at times a delay in escalation. This cannot be taught by a book, but my training programmes are built around improving this, like the aviation industry, and aim to strengthen communication, teach techniques in escalation and explore how individuals respond to stress. This is a fascinating aspect of teaching, learning and development and must be done in a supported and psychologically safe environment for staff. In our work, we teach our teams, especially the person who is leading, that they need to stand at the end of the bed, delegate specific interventions, so they can see the whole picture.

Stepping back to see the whole picture is a concept that I believe can be applied to all areas of life. Considering the different roles I hold in my life allows me to be comfortable with my own versions of myself. When I am at work, I am a consultant paediatrician, but when I am with my friends, I am the girlfriend, when I am with my husband, I am a wife, a partner, and when I am with my children, I am the mummy. At home, I am the softer version of myself, and I am able to relax and enjoy my time with my family.

We can so easily get swept up in the minutiae of everyday life and not remember to take a step back, breathe, and think about the bigger picture. Taking a step back at moments during the day allows us to put everything into perspective and move from tunnel vision to having a panoramic view.

ACKNOWLEDGMENTS

My networks have been a great source of influence and inspiration for me especially when I meet other authors who have written fantastic books sharing their unique gift with the world. Since writing my first book, Voices from Punjab with my co-author Aastha K Singhania, I uncovered great value in raising women's voices. It urged me to further my work with female empowerment.

The twenty-one magnificent women in this book have openly shared their stories, messages and life experience, giving us a unique insight. They have been vulnerable, inspirational, and broadened our perspective on life as a British Gujarati woman. My heartfelt gratitude towards these fabulous women: Nisha Parmar, Sonali Shah, Ameesha Bhudia, Panna Vekaria, Dr Yoge Patel, Shivali Bhammer, Hansa Pankania, Nishma Gosrani OBE, Minal Mehta, Naomi Dattani, Lavina Mehta MBE, Heena Shah, Nina Amin MBE, Trupti Patel, Varsha Mistry, Heeral Shah,

Kalpana Doshi, Kamu Palan, Chandni Vora, Krishna Pujara and Dr Trisha Radia.

I am hugely grateful for all the people that have encouraged me to self-publish this book so that it can be shared with the world even faster: Mirela Sula, Anil Gupta and Jo Davison. I am extremely blessed to have had support from Pinky Lilani CBE DL for introducing me to some of the incredible women after attending the annual Asian Women of Achievement awards in London.

I am very fortunate for the love and encouragement I receive from my parents and siblings for the work that I love doing- sharing powerful stories and elevating women's voices.

My heartfelt gratitude towards my amazing husband, for always standing by me, lifting my spirit and for being my greatest champion. Without Avnish's faith and dedication to our relationship, I would not have written this book. He adds value to me and all the surrounding communities in our collective work in social care, education, and the charity sector. Thank you!

THE AUTHOR

Anita Goyal is the Chair of the Hemraj Goyal Foundation as well as a renowned author (*Voices from Punjab, Troubador Publishing*), an award-winning philanthropist, a chair and trustee of many charitable organisations and foundations and the host of the podcast Relight Your Fire.

Anita's career began as a teacher in an all-girls school in inner-city London, and her mission has remained unchanged: to promote the education of key social issues, empower women and children around the globe, collaborate with organisations driving critical social change and set the stage for a new generation of far-reaching philanthropy.

Marrying the entrepreneur and philanthropist Avnish Goyal introduced Anita to the world of philanthropy and gave her the opportunity to utilise her passion and skills for education on a much larger scale, including becoming the CEO and Chair of the Hemraj Goyal Foundation, which partners with more than 30 different charities and organisations every year.

Anita's sits on the Board of Trustees of the Hallmark Care Homes Foundation, holds the position of Vice President of Barnardo's and is an ambassador of the Alzheimer's Society alongside her involvement with a number of other related charities. In 2014, she launched Ultimate You, an organisation delivering educational personal development workshops and seminars, with her husband.

Anita and Avnish's energy and drive over the years has been recognised through a number of awards. Most recently, Anita received an MBE from the Queen in the annual New Year's Honours list for her services in diversity and female empowerment, attracting widespread media coverage.

Anita is continually looking for new ways to empower and educate communities all over the world and, under her guidance, the foundations she runs have had a profound impact in the charity and social care sectors. Her passion for helping people has led to numerous initiatives and programmes. Her vision for social change will continue to inspire and impact individuals and communities for years to come.

www.anitagoyal.com

Anita Goyal

Also by Anita Goyal

VOICES FROM PUNJAB

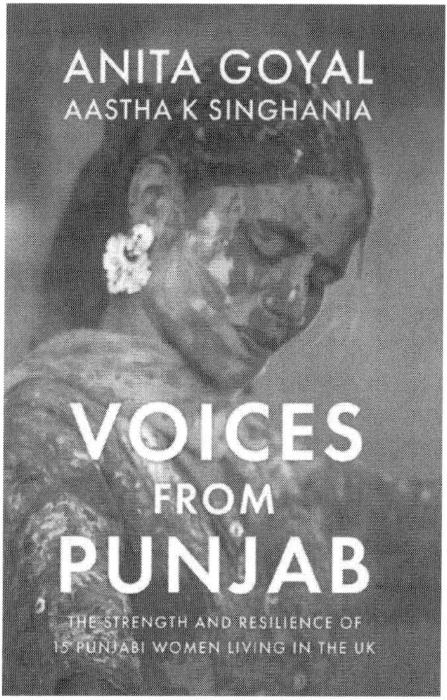

A charity book sponsored by The Hemraj Goyal Foundation (hgf.org.uk) to help support vulnerable women and education for girls living in Punjab, India.

HEMRAJ GOYAL
FOUNDATION

Made in the USA
Columbia, SC
05 March 2022

57224254R00211